Advance praise for *Transitions of the Heart*

"For every thriving transgender or gender nonconforming son or daughter, there is a parent who has struggled, searched, listened, and loved. Rachel Pepper's *Transitions of the Heart* is a compelling and moving compilation of the personal stories of mothers from all walks of life who have taken that journey. In their own words, the mothers poignantly teach us one easy lesson: listen to your children, love them, and carve a path for their unique gender selves. Balancing a fierce love for their child against the fear of the challenges their child may face in a transphobic world, the mothers that Rachel Pepper so brilliantly brings to us in *Transitions of the Heart* give us an opportunity to know from the inside out what it takes to raise a healthy gender nonconforming or transgender son or daughter. The first book of its kind, it is a must-read for a~ ~ ~ho is a parent, works with a parent, or wan*~ ~ ~ ~ ~ mother's courage to overcome n~ ~ ~ ~ ~ ~ n unfriendly word, and stand ~ ~ ~ ~ ~ ~ ~

~ ~ ~ne Ehrensaft, PhD, author of ~ ~ ~ ~ ~ *Made* and Director of Mental H ~ ~ ~e Child and Adolescent Gender Center

"For many transgender or gender nonconforming people, our life journey is riddled with struggle, solitude, and a long road toward self-acceptance. The love from a mother is a treasured gift. *Transitions of the Heart* captures the complexity and depth of a mother's journey to understand and support her child—a child who, confronted with questions, fear, and self-doubt, is sometimes the one who leads the mother to understand the true meaning of unconditional love. The stories told in

Transitions of the Heart are brave, honest, compelling, and timely. They represent a powerful tool that can guide a parent from struggle to acceptance."

—The Jim Collins Foundation

"These honest, deeply felt testimonies of parents discovering and grappling with the unexpected difference of their trans child exemplify the grace of parental love. I am moved to tears reading these stories, amazed continually by the insight, tender reflection, and courageous love that each parent exhibits in their struggle to understand their trans child, and to parent responsibly and with inspiration. The book *Transitions of the Heart* restores my faith in the world."

—Max Wolf Valerio,
author of *The Testosterone Files*

"As a mother it's easy to relate to the concerns expressed by the contributors to Rachel Pepper's new book *Transitions of the Heart*. These mothers represent a variety of family arrangements, life stages, and backgrounds...but they communicate the love for their children, hope for their future, and self-doubt of their parenting skills familiar to most mothers. What happens when parents learn their child is transgender? How is it different if they are adults, or still in school? Will they be safe? Can they be happy? While the experiences are specific to being the mother of a transgender child, any mother can relate to the feelings the women reveal. The mothers we meet in these pages can be our friends, our neighbors, ourselves."

—Eden Lane,
host and producer of *In Focus* on Colorado Public Television

Transitions of the Heart

Transitions of the Heart

STORIES OF LOVE, STRUGGLE AND ACCEPTANCE BY MOTHERS OF TRANSGENDER AND GENDER VARIANT CHILDREN

Rachel Pepper

Foreword by Kim Pearson

CLEiS
PRESS

Published in the United States by Cleis Press Inc., 2246 Sixth Street, Berkeley CA 94710.
Printed in the United States.
Cover design: Scott Idleman/Blink
Cover photograph: ballyscanlon/Getty Images
Text design: Frank Wiedemann
10 9 8 7 6 5 4 3 2 1

Trade paper ISBN: 978-1-57344-788-1
E-book ISBN: 978-1-57344-801-7

Library of Congress Cataloging-in-Publication Data

Transitions of the heart : stories of love, struggle and acceptance by mothers of transgender and gender variant children / [edited by] Rachel Pepper.
p. cm.
ISBN 978-1-57344-788-1 (pbk. : alk. paper)
1. Parents of transsexuals. 2. Transgender children--Family relations. 3. Trans-sexuals--Family relations. 4. Gender identity. 5. Mother and child. I. Pepper, Rachel.

HQ77.9.T725 2012
306.874--dc23

2012002124

For all the mothers whose love and acceptance fills these pages and blazes a trail of courage for others to follow.
This book is for you and, of course, for your children.

Contents

Foreword

Kim Pearson

My transition of the heart began June 6, 2006. My severely depressed fourteen-year-old daughter and I had been working with a counselor twice a week for six months. I remember nearly every detail of that afternoon: the uncharacteristic confidence in my child's walk; the upright posture; the calm demeanor and direct eye contact. You see, that day my child began to walk in truth and the truth was that I never had a daughter. At the end of the hour I exited the office knowing I had a son.

It is difficult to explain the sense of isolation parents raising a gender nonconforming child often experience. Many endure the disapproving gaze or comments of strangers in the grocery store. Family members may criticize their parenting skills and occasionally they are reported to social service agencies for alleged abuse of their children. Then there is the particular struggle of the parents that didn't see any signs of gender nonconformity in their young children. They are taken totally off guard when their children assert their cross-gender identity and it's quite a struggle to make sense of this situation.

No one ever tells you that having a transgender child is a possibility. It isn't in any of the baby or child-rearing books. How can anyone be prepared for this journey? It's as if we have been forced into running a marathon and all the other runners are given a five-mile lead and a map of the course. We spend our time trying to catch up, with no idea if we are even on the right path.

We want facts and figures. We want information on how to keep our children safe. We want to know our children will be happy and successful. We want to know that we have not lost our minds and that someone truly understands what we are going through.

On that day in 2006, I went looking for the information I needed to help my child and I discovered a startling void. No books, no articles, no websites, nothing that directly related to children who were like my son. What I did eventually find was a group of courageous parents traveling the same road. We talked, cried, ranted, grieved, and comforted each other. We gave each other hope. After hope came inspiration and after inspiration came action.

Along with two other mothers I began to tell my story more publicly. We helped other families like ours find and support each other. We learned that by sharing our stories we were changing hearts and minds. Our journeys are as distinct as the personalities of our children. Magic is created when we come together and share our joys and challenges with each other and with the world. Today there are websites, television shows, documentaries, blogs, and books. We are filling the void with our voices.

Rachel Pepper's new anthology, *Transitions of the Heart: Stories of Love, Struggle and Acceptance by Mothers of Transgender and Gender Variant Children*, provides intimate glimpses into the joys, challenges, and triumphs of families like ours. It is a support group, a tutorial, and an educational text all rolled into one. In my work with families, schools, and communities, I have found that it is rarely a person's mind that must be changed, but rather their heart. Whether you are a parent, educator, health-care professional, or just generally interested in this topic, be prepared for these stories to change your heart. And there can be no better person to compile such a collection than Rachel, whose dedicated work as a therapist and as a writer makes her uniquely qualified to advocate for families such as ours.

Inspiring others to see that our transgender children are gifts to the world is my daily goal. I am truly grateful to have a collection such as *Transitions of the Heart* to add to my toolbox and to recommend to others.

Namaste,
Kim Pearson

Executive Director/Co-founder, TransYouth Family Allies
(Proud mom of Shawn, who taught our family so much about love, truth and understanding; you are my greatest teacher.)

Introduction

Rachel Pepper

As a therapist and as the co-author of *The Transgender Child: A Handbook for Families and Professionals* (written with Stephanie Brill), I know very well that there are few professionally published resources for mothers of transgender and gender nonconforming people.

Transitions of the Heart was conceived to focus on the emotional experience of mothers, highlighting the parallel process that parents go through along with their transitioning child.

For as children transition, so too must their families, and no one feels this change as acutely as mothers, who often both bear their children and act as their primary caretakers. The bond between mothers and their children is one that is frequently referenced, but too infrequently spoken of honestly. What do mothers really think about their transgender and gender variant children? It was my goal to find out.

The mothers you will meet in this book come from all walks of life, and are diverse in ethnicity, race, national origin, and class. They are birth mothers and adoptive mothers, single mothers and married mothers, stepmothers and grandmothers, and heterosexual mothers and lesbian mothers. They have children of all ages, ranging from age six to about age sixty, with just about every age in between. Their children are gender nonconforming, gender variant, gender queer, transgender, and "pink boys." Many mothers are active in PFLAG groups and/or in both online and community-based, peer-led support groups for parents of transgender and gender nonconforming children.

I found most of my authors as a result of a wide-ranging call for submissions through both national and international email listservs. Others were referred to the project by friends or their transgender children. Only a few were known to me before I began the book. Out of all the mothers, only a handful have ever written professionally or been published before. Indeed, several are telling their stories here for the first time. Most are willing to be published using their real names. Others, concerned for the privacy of their families or specifically their children, are using pseudonyms. Their stories have touched me deeply, and many have made me cry, even in repeated readings. Through the very gift of their stories, I feel I have become friends with these mothers, and I hope after reading their pieces, you will feel the same way.

The mothers in this book have struggled to understand the gender identity of their children as best as they could.

And for the most part, they have come out the other side of this struggle with love and acceptance. Along the way, they have felt many strong emotions and grappled with questions that few had immediate answers for. They have had to advocate, educate, and protect their kids from spouses, ex-partners, family members, school administrators, neighbors, teachers, coaches, pediatricians, psychiatrists, therapists, communities of faith, and every other variety of institution that supposedly exists to support children and families. In short, these mothers are very busy changing the world!

Indeed, the mothers in this book have already blazed a brave trail for those who follow. They have spoken out, changed policies and legislation, and are continuing to act as leaders in their families and communities for the safety and acceptance of all children, everywhere.

They have challenged school leaders to make restrooms accessible for transgender teens. They have walked with their young children into school classrooms the first time their children wore a gender-confirming outfit. They have allowed their "pink boys" to wear skirts to family gatherings and on national TV. They have grappled with the complexity of changing pronouns, and they have learned to call their children by new names after the ones they chose so carefully at birth were rejected or became obsolete. Their stories are full of the struggle, love, and acceptance they face today and everyday. We all have much to learn from them.

The idea for this book was inspired by the success of the Cleis Press title, *Different Daughters: A Book by Mothers of Lesbians*. Originally published in 1987 and edited by Louise Rafkin, *Different Daughters* has gone through many printings and has had an amazing and long-lasting impact on both the field of LGBT studies and in the real lives of families everywhere. One of the first books of its kind, *Different Daughters* set a precedent of connectedness, clarity, honesty, and self-reflection for families with LGBT children, long before the current proliferation of in-person and online support groups. In a flash of insight, Cleis understood that it would be timely to do a similar book, this time by the mothers of transgender children.

I'd like to thank everyone who helped make this anthology bloom into a book we could all be proud of. To those who helped get the word out into cyberspace about this project, especially the administrators of various listservs for parents of transgender children, you have my deepest appreciation. To all the mothers who queried me and especially those whose pieces made it into the book, thank you for trusting me with your stories and your lives. I have tried to honor your integrity as best I could, for I have the deepest respect for your courage in helping shape a new, better world for people of all genders. My thanks also go to Cleis Press for conceiving of, believing in, and publishing this project. Thanks to Kim Pearson of Trans Youth Family Allies, herself a tireless advocate for transgender children, for writing the foreword. And finally, thanks to my partner Kellen for so many reasons, and then some.

Rachel Pepper
Oakland, California

Sean

Nancy Moore

I didn't see him coming. I didn't have a little girl who looked or acted in any way like a boy, and my early-adolescent Sarah was tiny, with flowing hair, painted nails, and a continuous stream of boyfriends. Sarah was a little sister, the younger of my two daughters, a niece, a granddaughter.

I'm writing this essay while looking at two pictures of the same person. One is an old picture of Sarah when she was thirteen years old, her beautiful self smiling back at me. Next to this picture is one of my son, before testosterone, but after coming out as transgender. This is a photograph of my wonderful boy, now with short hair, the same big, brown eyes, wearing his signature leather jacket and looking into the camera with confidence and a broad grin—someone I would not have missed knowing for anything in the world.

When Sarah was seventeen, I picked her up from an out-of-state summer arts program and watched her say good-bye to a friend who addressed her as "Sean." *Sean.* This was the first time I had heard the name my child had chosen for himself, and it is probably not an exaggeration to say that at that moment a tectonic plate shifted under my feet.

Acknowledging this name was important, I knew. But I was in complete panic, and it was like that for a while as Sean patiently (and not so patiently) educated me about what he had been experiencing and what he knew to be true about himself. He also had certain requests, one of them being that I say "he," "him," and "his" when referring to him. For some parents, "mastering the pronouns" may feel enormously challenging, but by using these identifiers, I feel like I have won Sean's respect.

I was very active in my children's lives, yet Sean's transgender world was something I refused to educate myself about, at first. I shied away from reading or watching anything on the subject of gender identity. I didn't look into support groups or seek out parents of transgender children. Yet when someone suggested that Sean's identity was "just a phase," with the intention of consoling me, my back went up, and I found myself defending my new son and praising his courage.

I was counting on my child to guide me. He seemed to be educating everyone around him, all the time, yet this was a lot to ask of such a young person who was only just learning who he was. To have to blaze a trail as trans in an inner-city high school, in addition to educating his own parents, must have been very difficult for him. But Sean was a good and able teacher. And so it seems especially poignant that he is now in graduate school studying to be a teacher. He is also an activist for transgender rights.

Does the path from birth to transgender ever follow a straight line? Sarah had come out as a lesbian at age fifteen. We were all sitting around the Thanksgiving table at my mother's house. I had recently divorced my husband of twenty years, and we were spending this day with my extended family. Sarah sat to my left and her big sister to my right.

Toward the end of the meal, Sarah climbed onto my lap and asked if we could go around the table and each say what we were most thankful for. As her turn approached, she said something about school, yet I could feel her petite frame vibrating with emotion. When everyone was done, she grabbed her sister's hand under the table, took a deep breath, and asked, in a wobbly voice, if we could go around the table again because someone might have left something out.

Everyone became quiet as we each, again, found something to be grateful for, waiting for what was obviously something important from Sarah. This time around, she said that she was grateful that her parents had "come out" as unhappy in their marriage, because this gave her permission to come out as gay. The table was stunned into silence for only a brief moment, and then my family rose from their seats to hug her.

I was dazed, but not confused. Through all the boyfriends and the lipstick and the sparkly nail polish, something had been transpiring for Sarah in middle school. She experienced a kind of persecution that was too ugly for her to talk about for much of the time. There was a rumored girlfriend among her succession of boyfriends. Former friends taunted and tortured her.

She and I talked about so many things, yet this area seemed too tender to probe. Looking back, I can't figure out whether this sensitivity was mine or hers.

Sarah was "out" now, but something hard to name was still deeply out of reach for me. What I didn't realize at the time was that this *something* was really a *someone*. It was Sean, and Sean was most definitely within reach for my daughter.

She found him by listening to that voice that so many of us have learned to ignore amid the din of expectation and assumption. I was ignoring what was probably screaming at me as Sarah experimented with her hair, which was the most visible and perhaps safest way she could express her gender identity. The long hair became a bob, then a Mohawk. We went shopping for clothing in the boys' department. I came to understand that her clothing was not a costume, not something she was trying on for size, and that her female parts were not a secret she was keeping. She was bending gender.

I could be an ally in this process that had no name, or I could be someone to avoid. I chose to keep my focus on my child and not on the larger implications and issues. Sarah slowly built a second family of support in a "trans-friendly" community nearby and made abiding friendships there. Yet I didn't feel supplanted. Mostly what I felt was grateful.

When Sean turned eighteen, he decided to go on testosterone as he left for college. He had been seeing a therapist and was excited to take the next steps in establishing his identity. I was terrified of talking with him about this, instead asking myself the question that had become all too familiar: Will I say the wrong thing and lose communication and trust?

I went ahead anyway, reminding myself that we were

both sailing in uncharted waters. I asked whether using testosterone for decades might lead to major health complications and perhaps even premature death. His answer was one of the more poignant things a mother can hear from her child: "I'd rather die than have to live any other way."

For me, one of the hardest things about Sean's transition has been the loss of Sarah. I have experienced deep grief about this, and I would continue to do so if not for the experience of my friends who have actually lost children to illness or accident. That perspective has been invaluable. And it is not lost on me that for his part, Sean still willingly and lovingly recognizes me through all my many changes.

The hard part is right there when I am confronted with a flooded basement and discover that early photos of Sarah have been destroyed. I have saved old phone messages that Sean, pre-testosterone, has left me. These are rare echoes of a sound I will not hear again. Along with testosterone come permanent changes—in voice, in body, in personality—and I don't want to lose the evidence that Sean existed in another form.

It is probably that reluctance to let go of Sarah that comes to me in my dreams, for she often appears in my dreams. At first, these "sightings" were extremely upsetting, but now I recognize them as part of my own transition. Nothing prepares the parent of a transgender child, and nothing prepares that child. For me, that's the good news: there's no rulebook.

It's hard to write about all of this, mostly because it feels like I'm unpacking a huge suitcase full of unopened letters I have not wanted to read. Recently, though, I've found opportunities to use my voice, this essay being one of them. I've also discovered an amazing group of parents of transgender children who meet regularly, a place where I can have a direct experience of how common and how utterly divergent our experiences have been on this parental path. And yet another major opportunity to "come out" as the parent of a transgender child was one I made for myself: I conceived the idea of an art exhibition entitled *Continuum: Gender Identities,* and curated it for a local gallery. The show included fifty-three artists from around the world, working in a wide range of media, expressing themselves on the subject of gender. The event encouraged the "big conversation in a small town" that I was craving, and the reception and publicity it received was overwhelmingly positive. All these opportunities to express support for my child tell me that, finally, I'm ready to unpack the suitcase.

What I keep coming back to in my head is that there is nothing "wrong" with my child. There is everything right with discovering the core of yourself—something that so few people, of either gender, manage to accomplish.

Those questions of what I could have done differently, and whether I caused my child to be transgender, diminish both me as a parent and Sean as the magnificent person he is. My son is here and now, and I am too.

Nancy Moore is a working artist, and a book editor and proofreader. Moore is an artist member of the Silvermine Guild of Artists in New Canaan, and is on the board of the Ridgefield Guild of Artists in Connecticut. She is the proud mother of her two heroes, Emily and Sean.

Discovering Raffi

Marion Freedman-Gurspan

I used to talk about my son. As she transitioned, I began to use the word *child,* avoiding the gender marker altogether. Now I talk about my daughter.

When I was forty-two, I applied to adopt a child from Honduras because it was one of the very few countries willing to place an infant with an older single Jewish woman. I didn't know if I would be assigned a boy or girl, or whether the child would be of Spanish, Caribbean black, or indigenous Indian background, or a mix. I had my first date with my husband-to-be the day that I dropped the adoption application in the mail. We brought Rafael home two years later when he was 9 months old, and we married ten days after that.

Creating opportunities for Raffi to find his own identity

and to be comfortable in a variety of circumstances has been a motif in my life. I got to name him shortly after his birth, and selected a name that was American enough but that respected his Honduran heritage. This name was Rafael. I moved to a town with excellent schools, a racially and ethnically diverse population, and a good deli. Our family was delighted to see a new baby. The extended family includes the four children from my husband's first marriage, encompasses biological and adopted children, whites and blacks, Jews and non-Jews, and those born both here and abroad.

Raffi was raised with the Marlo Thomas video, *Free to Be You and Me*, which was created to break through gender stereotypes. Raffi says that I was raised with those same values, and therefore I was just following my family's tradition. We allowed him to follow his inclinations. He played with Barbie dolls. He disliked sports but loved plays and music and dancing and museums of all kinds. He liked history books, but preferred reading books about girls, such as the American Girl series. He was tiny, smiley, and easy going, so the boys at school protected him and the girls mothered him.

At the end of sixth grade, a neighbor asked if I knew that Raffi was telling students at school that he was gay. I replied that I wasn't aware he was saying anything about his sexuality, but I wasn't surprised or upset. There was only one serious bullying incident involved with this disclosure, and that got swiftly addressed.

Although I was not concerned when Raffi entered a public high school as an openly gay student, that calm quickly passed. Raffi had affiliated himself with the Gay Straight Alliance, and one of the teachers asked him if he would speak to a group of students who had had a history of substance abuse or delinquency problems. The intent was well-founded, but the effort failed on all counts. The students weren't prepared, nor was Raffi informed about the possible consequences of coming out to a group with less-than-ideal social skills. After speaking, he was labeled by the whole school as "that gay kid" and became a target for hallway taunts. My husband and I met with the dean to stress the school's responsibility for protecting vulnerable students. The episode was both frightening and enlightening. I learned how much fear and hatred there was out there. I learned how labels stick. And I learned that I needed to teach Raffi to watch out for himself, always evaluating the risk of homophobic violence. Gone was my middle-class illusion of safety.

Although I didn't see it at the time, Raffi's self-realization and transition to womanhood began in high school. He attended many trainings on sexual orientation and gender identity, and spent hours on the internet exploring these issues. Raffi kept talking to me about being two-spirited, having both a feminine and masculine spirit. This is an acknowledged identity in several Native American and other indigenous cultures around the world. In response, I would nod and agree that the description seemed to fit him, but he kept the gay label.

When Raffi decided he wanted to become the only male cheerleader at the high school, we supported his effort to make the squad; when he was selected, my husband, mother, and I attended games and cheered with everyone else. He was finally accepted for himself, and only one of the football players openly made gay slurs. Raffi seemed to do well as a shy gay teen, having a few female friends, a few crushes on guys, and going to school dances as well as gay dances, but dating neither boys nor girls.

When Raffi went off to a small Midwestern college as an openly gay man of color, we all felt he would be happy and safe there. I was glad that he would have a chance to grow up and explore his identity away from my vigilant eyes. We established the pattern I had with my parents of once-a-week phone calls, unless something urgent came up. Raffi, still only five foot one, became fast friends with a group of very large football players and was well-liked at school.

I was caught completely off-guard the first time I saw Raffi dressed as a woman. We came to visit him during his sophomore year, spent a day together, and then, when we met later for dinner with a group of his friends, Raffi appeared in a skirt and heels. He had said nothing. Since none of his friends seemed surprised, we knew this was not a first-time event. I felt a thud in my heart, then took a deep breath. My husband and I looked at each other, and acknowledged what we had seen. We felt bad that Raffi had felt unable to tell us beforehand, but there was no need to ask what this was about. We knew.

I sent a son abroad for his junior year of college. When Raffi flew home in mid-winter for my mother's funeral, he had long hair and was wearing make-up. Some of my friends commented on how beautiful and relaxed she looked. By the time we visited Norway in May, we were visiting a daughter. Raffi lived her senior year at college as a woman, learning to fight for her rights as a transgender person as she sought the housing she wanted. Our daughter now lives with us and has succeeded in finding part-time professional work that may be leading to some full-time options.

As a mother, I worry. I worry about her getting a decent job, but mostly, I worry about her social life. Will Raffi find truly good friends? I worry that she will have superficial friends, but not close ones. Will she find a partner, a man to live with, ideally someone to raise a family with? Raffi faced one horrible experience in college when the close friends from the football team decided they didn't want to be associated with a transgender woman, rejected her as a housemate, and spurned her on campus. It took her a while to recover, and I hope she has the resilience and support to keep going should this happen again.

Raffi navigates the world as a woman, and is thoughtful about the places she goes and how she gets there. I am sad that although Raffi would like to contribute to development in Honduras as a teacher or by doing community development work, she probably never will because transgender people are frequently victimized there. She has traveled to her birthplace with us, but would not be safe traveling or living there on her own. I am sad that so many situations require negotiating. I am sad that before going to a swimming pool she has to think about the shower and locker room set-up.

I am truly grateful for the things I do not have to worry about. Relatives on both sides of the family are completely accepting of her. Our friends are accepting. We belong to a synagogue that is accepting. We live in a state that, while it has yet to pass protections for transgender people, does have protections for gays and lesbians.

Most of all, I am happy that Raffi still has her bright eyes and her smile. She is the same child I have always known and loved.

Marion Freedman-Gurspan is a retired social worker who directed policy and program development for children with serious emotional disturbance and their families for the Massachusetts Department of Mental Health. She now advocates for the rights of individuals who are transgender. She lives in Brookline with her husband and her daughter Raffi.

Dear Friends and Family: A Letter About My Daughter

Barbara Gurr

Dear Friends and Family:

I apologize for sending you all a crazy form letter, but our family has news to share! And it's so hard sometimes to get together that we thought we'd send a letter to those people who mean the most to us, and let you in on what's going on with us.

The news we have is kind of hard to share, and after thinking and praying about it for a while, it seems best to send a letter for two reasons: we have to start letting people know what's going on with us, and it might be easier for some people to get a letter they can react to honestly and privately—without worrying about hurting our feelings, or saying the "right" thing (whatever *that* is) or the "wrong" thing (whatever *that* is).

As some of you have no doubt begun to notice over the last couple of years (especially if you've spent time with us more recently), Thomas is presenting us with a bit of a surprise. Our son Thomas is transgender. This means that although he was born with boy parts, he's really a she. What's on the outside does not match what's on the inside of him. He's been telling us this in his own way for years—literally since he could talk—and we have finally begun to really listen to our child.

Thomas is a girl. This is hard for us, and we have no doubt that this revelation will be hard for many of you to accept, as well. That's okay. We know you love us and want the best for us—that's why you're getting this letter. We want you to understand what this means so that we can all be honest with each other about our concerns and our fears. Certainly, we have plenty of those.

Let me provide you with some background. The Christmas before Thomas turned three, he and I were toy shopping, and we strolled past the "girls" aisle. It felt like Thomas had been lost at sea, and suddenly had found the mother ship. He insisted on going down this aisle and was thrilled with everything in it. That Christmas he got a pink stroller and a doll from Santa, and it was a wonderful Christmas for him. Since then, he's shown a marked preference for all things girly, and, in fact, rejects the toys his older brother plays with.

By the time Thomas was almost five, this was a very clear preference, and my husband was especially concerned. But we tried to consider this a positive thing: our son could express all sides of being human without rejecting the things

14

that we consider "feminine."

However, by his fifth Christmas, his preference had become an issue—he was playing dress-up with the neighbors and in my clothes, and continually wanted to put make-up on me and do my hair. (You all know I don't wear make-up or style my hair, so this was a new, and frankly annoying, experience for me.) Thomas had no friends who were boys, but was quite popular with girls. When it was time to buy a bike two summers ago, he wanted a pink princess bike with a frilly basket. He wouldn't even look at the other bikes. So although it was hard for my husband, that's the bike he bought. A bike seemed like such a small thing on which to give in, and Thomas was so happy with it.

But that Christmas, right before he turned five, Thomas didn't get anything girly. We didn't buy him anything girly for his birthday in January, either. A few months later, he confessed that it had been a very sad Christmas for him, because he didn't get anything he wanted, and he didn't know why. Thomas asked me why Santa didn't like him anymore, and began to cry. This is when things really started to turn for me, and, I suspect, for my husband as well. Holding my child while he cried, I thought, well, we would never do that again.

We worried about sending Thomas to kindergarten this past fall. When I took the kids back-to-school shopping, Thomas chose a pink, sparkly backpack. I went back to the store later to buy him a compromise backpack that is a more subtle purple and black, and convinced him that the pink, sparkly backpack would be good for hiking and traveling, but was too big for school. Actually, both backpacks are the same size, and I have done a lot of this moderately deceitful maneuvering out of my desire to protect him—and it's becoming unbearable for me. Of course his parents are the very people Thomas should be able to trust without question.

Thomas has done really well in school—very good grades, lots of friends (all girls), and a teacher we really like. Several things have developed, however, that have pushed this issue forward for us. The first was the self-portrait Thomas drew on the first day of school. He pictured himself in a big, poofy dress with long hair. At this point, it occurred to us that virtually all his drawings are of girls. Dressing up also increased in the early fall, as did his interest in girly TV shows and movies. At the same time, he's never been interested in sports, and our efforts to get him to play soccer and t-ball have failed miserably. By mid-fall, we knew we needed some guidance.

In school, Thomas has fully identified himself as a girl to his classmates. Everyone knows it, and after the initial confusion, everyone seems to have accepted it. We don't know how long this grace period will last, but for now, school is fine. We've had numerous conversations with the school about this, and although they're struggling a bit with how to keep Thomas safe from bullying (which has not happened), they also need to keep other families and parents in mind. We understand that this is a tricky situation for the school, and we're trying to be patient with them as they figure it all out. Overall, the school has been very good.

This past fall I enrolled in a class at the university called the Sociology of Sexualities to help me with this. While the class didn't cover childhood gender issues, it did give me some insight into adult gender and transgender identities. I also contacted a local organization that works with sexual minority adolescents (gay, lesbian, bisexual, transgender, and much more), and they gave me some contact information for a few therapists in our state. None of these people work with children Thomas's age; they all work with adults and adolescents (when sexuality begins to really develop). Thomas has shown absolutely no signs of anxiety, depression, or stress over this, but we want to be on top of things as he develops.

We eventually went to see a therapist who asked us several questions about Thomas: were his friends predominantly boys or girls? What were his favorite play activities? What were the things that made him smile? When we told her that every picture Thomas has ever drawn of himself is as a girl, that he prefers to pee sitting down "like mommy," and that it has always been this way, the therapist told us she was pretty confident that he's transgender. Less than a month later, we went to a second therapist. To tell you the truth, by then we were also thinking that Thomas is transgender, but—well, that's a scary thought. We weren't even sure what that meant, and we wanted to gather as much information as possible. I think we were both hoping that maybe the first therapist was wrong. But our second therapist agreed that Thomas is, in all likelihood, transgender.

A couple of weeks ago, we attended a support group for parents of transgender youth. Although all of the children of these parents are older than Thomas, it was very helpful and we're very grateful to have found it. This group is also providing a monthly art class for the kids themselves. I took Thomas a couple weeks ago, and although it was only Thomas and an eleven year old, he loved it.

The best resource may prove to be the third therapist we

just consulted last week. This woman is the only person we've been able to find who works with children Thomas's age. We really like her. She's a clinical psychologist with a long history of working with transgender issues. I brought Thomas down to meet her earlier this week and they really hit it off. After hearing our story and spending a couple of hours playing and chatting with Thomas, she confirmed that our child is transgender. But the truth is, we already knew this. In our hearts, we knew. We've continued to see this therapist, and I think she'll be very helpful for us as we move forward.

I want to stress that Thomas is not expressing any negative responses to any of these efforts. I think that this is largely due to the fact that we are really trying to keep him safe while also allowing him to be who he is. My mom and sister-in-law have been fabulously supportive, and it means so much to all of us that they create such safe and loving spaces for us. Also, Thomas has a few wonderful friends who understand that he's a girl, and whose parents (who deserve a real conversation about this soon) have not questioned us about these things.

Kids are so amazing; at school, they seem to just go with the flow. If Thomas prefers to draw unicorns and fairies and sit with the girls, no one seems to care. He gets plenty of play dates (all girls), and their usual activity is playing dress-up. A few friends have dropped off, and this has been sad for us, but no one has been overly aggressive or invasive about our decisions for Thomas.

Last week I made my first foray into the girls' clothing section of the local department store. I honestly think it was one of the hardest things I've had to do in this process. On one side of the aisle are all the boys' clothes, the clothes I've become so familiar with over the last several years. On the other side are all the girls' clothes, like a foreign landscape to me. Plus, girls' clothes are really quite complicated. The skirts are too short, and the boots have heels on them, for heaven's sake! Even the jeans are low-rise. My child is only six, and I'm looking at clothes I wouldn't buy for a fourteen-year-old!

Still, as hard as it was to buy these clothes, giving them to Thomas was the most amazingly wonderful experience. His sheer joy at getting jeans with flowers on the pockets and shirts with sparkly hearts just about broke my heart with love—as well as fear and concern. It struck me as he was doing a fashion show for us, trying on all of these clothes, that I honestly don't think I've ever seen him that fully happy. He's started to wear girls' shirts to school, and this week began wearing girl-style jeans. We're trying to move at a moderate pace, but honestly, Thomas has not just come out of the closet on this, he's blown the closet up. He's very happy and excited about all these new opportunities. I didn't think he was terribly unhappy before, but the difference in his demeanor, his smile, even his sleep has been remarkable.

Though I wasn't fully aware of his discontent, now everything seems to be going much more smoothly. Thomas is much more relaxed, and less shy with new people. He smiles more and hugs us more, and is happy to go visit family members. He has also decided that her new name is "Tonya" and we're all trying to remember this. Luckily, she's very patient with us when we forget.

Aside from our own fears and anxieties (which feel overwhelming most of the time), it's actually all been quite smooth, so far. Transitioning at school was made much easier by Tonya's teacher, with whom we're in regular contact. And the school administrators have been very supportive—even to the extent of seeking out professional guidance from a local organization. When we first went to the school, I literally had the phone number for the local ACLU in my back pocket. I was ready for a fight, telling myself "No one is going to deny my child. No one is going to hurt my kid." But the school staff has been nothing but compassionate. I think they already sensed something different about Thomas and were just waiting for us to come in and talk to them. We all cried a little bit at that initial meeting, as my husband and I shared our fears and our love for our child. But the school principal, assistant principal, nurse, and Thomas's teacher reassured us that they were there to help and keep all the children in their school safe.

Our neighbors also got right on board. Again, they probably already sensed something was going on, since Thomas is over there playing dress-up with their daughters all the time. Even our pastor, a fairly conservative but loving man, told us, "God loves all his children. We can do no less." I had already been telling my husband I was prepared to leave our church and find something more progressive, but again, I was surprised and so very grateful. I won't lie, it's been a little awkward when we run errands around town and see parents with whom we haven't had a chance to discuss this. Thomas is dressed as a girl and truly passes as a girl, but they of course know Thomas as a boy. Still, other than a few raised eyebrows, no one has challenged us.

Thomas's older brother has transitioned very easily into seeing Thomas as "part-girl and part-boy," and we're keeping an eye on his reactions in order to make sure we can provide him with any help or guidance he may need. He loves Thomas very much and is very protective of him. His friends have also been pretty cool with this so far—one of them even refers to Thomas as his new "little sister." We all know children can be cruel at times, but these kids have been so wonderfully flexible and kind.

The most important thing for transgender children is that they know they are loved and accepted no matter who they are. They're just like every other child, except that their inside doesn't "match" their outside. No one is certain why this is, or how it happens—and at this point, that doesn't matter. What matters is that Tonya knows she's loved. We're very fortunate to have such loving family and friends around us who can make sure she never doubts this.

We have no idea where all of this will go. However, the studies, the therapists, and the books all agree that gender, including transgender identity, is pretty firmly settled for kids by the time they're between ages five and seven. So if Tonya says he's a she—well, she probably is. We undoubtedly have a long and challenging road ahead for us to keep our baby safe and strong. Most days we're terrified, and on the days in between we're exhausted.

We know that this is difficult news to receive in a letter, and we want you to know that we're communicating this news in this way for three reasons: we love you; we know you love us; and we just don't see each other often enough to be able to have a face-to-face conversation about this. It's very likely that the next time we see each other, Tonya could be wearing a skirt, so we want you to be as prepared as possible, and we appreciate so very much your support of our family.

Much love,
Our Family

> *Barbara Gurr is a feminist sociologist at a large university in the Northeast. Her research is in genders, sexualities, reproduction, and the body. She is the proud mother of six-year-old Tonya and her awesome older brother who are learning, as Barb is, that genders and sexualities are complicated, but love doesn't have to be.*

A Hard Road

Mary Lou Houle

I want to say right up front that this has been a long, hard road for me. Generally, I don't like to talk about myself, and, after all, this is really about my son's life.

The whole time my child was growing up, I never understood why he was always so angry, or how he could be so mean to me. He was always abrupt, sarcastic, talked back to me, and treated me as though I just didn't know anything. I felt that somehow I had done something wrong, and I didn't know what it was. I had three other sons; they seemed "normal" and he didn't. But I guess that was simply because he wasn't like them.

I will only use the pronoun *he* in this story because that is what my son wants. Now I like and love my son, but that was not always the case. He was my child and I loved him, but I did not like him.

I am the oldest of five siblings. My parents were both German and came directly from Germany. I was born in 1930 and we were poor by today's standards. I have a Lutheran background and a very strict childhood upbringing. So when I got married I knew I would love my children and they would know it by my love and my actions.

My story is about my first child born in 1952. He was born a girl, and the next three were boys. During my children's early years, I was dealing with a divorce, and that was very painful for me. I learned from the Bible that divorce is a sin, so I was sure that I was no longer loved by God, which added to my stress.

When my oldest child reached the fifth grade, mothers were invited to come to school with their children for a program about the changes in their bodies. The presenters talked about female issues like periods and ovulation. When we came home from that meeting, my child threw all the books in the fireplace and said, "I will never do that!" and never did. In fact, because I was concerned that he had never started to menstruate, I took him to our family doctor and he put him on birth control pills. This did start his menstruation, but as soon as the pills were used up, he went off them, and he did not menstruate again. He was mad at me for making him go to the doctor in the first place, so I did not make him go back. That was the first clue I had that something was different about my child.

During his school years, my child participated in every sport he could, and was very good at all of them. He graduated from high school, went to college, and joined the Air Force. One day, when he was on leave, we went out to lunch and he announced that he had something to tell me. The way he was acting, I just knew it was the "gay thing," and that he just could not tell me. So I said, "If you are trying to tell me you are gay, I already figured that out." Then I told him it didn't matter to me, and he was relieved and surprised. After all, he never carried a purse, used any makeup, and had always been a real tomboy. And when he was little, he never played with dolls, only trucks and baseballs, stereotypical boy things. A mother just knows! I told him it made no difference to me and that I had known for some time. As far as family goes, most just commented that he had always looked more boy than girl anyway, and to most of them, it made no difference.

Years passed and he did Ironman Triathlons, one every year, and other races in between. I went to thirteen of them to cheer him on. A few years ago, he sat me down with my sister with whom he is close, and told us that he was really a man and had started the transition to be one. As he told us his story, I began to understand why he was the way he was. You have to go through a life like this to know what I mean. He seemed calm and sure of what he was doing, and very noticeably, his anger was gone. It was a shock at first, but then everything fit into place—his obsession with sports and his always living on the edge, so busy with all his races and activities. Since I just wanted him to be happy, it seemed to be a very good sign.

As I thought about all of this over the next few days, I realized that I had lost a daughter and gained another son. I shed a few tears over that. I asked him if he was happy and he said yes. Well, for many years that was all that I had been praying for, because he had always been so angry.

Now this was a whole different thing as far as family was concerned. Some thought he was out of his mind I guess, and at the same time some thought it was okay—at least that is what they said to me. Of course, I realize that sometimes people say what they think you want to hear. Me on the other hand... It has been a hard road, but I am truly happy now because my son is happy. We are closer now than we have ever been, and see each other at least twice a year, spending two or three weeks together. He comes here or I go there. We find we can now joke with each other. We laugh and we have long talks. That never happened before!

When I turned seventy-five, my new son Sam managed to get the whole family to church on my birthday, and it was a total surprise. He worked a year on that surprise and involved my pastor and the church's secretary. People came from all over the US. I always knew he loved me, but now he was able to show his love.

Parents, I would say only this: love your children, no matter what. God gave them to you and they have a right to be happy, well-adjusted people. I know this because I have lost two sons—one was in an accident and the other committed suicide—and I would do anything to have them back with me. I think when you lose a child, your values change. I believe that the Holy Spirit brought me back to my faith through the son that committed suicide. My church supports me in so many ways and no one judges me there.

What I am realizing now is that my oldest son and I had many years of not connecting, and now we are finally able to.

So, I will treasure every minute that I have left. At my age, it feels like I won't have enough time to enjoy him. But don't get me wrong, I do plan on being around for a long time yet!

Mary Lou Houle lives in Ohio and is eighty years old. She credits her doctor and her son with keeping her in good health. She believes that her background helps her stay compassionate and always stick up for the underdog.

A Twin Story

Melissa McLaren

Nothing prepares you for having identical twins. One second you're in the doctor's office thinking you're in the middle of a miscarriage, and the next you've got your head between your knees taking deep breaths trying to make the leap from no babies to two of them. Motherhood can be like that—a never-ending roller coaster of adapting your expectations with the needs of your family.

Despite their appearance, my children have always been very different from each other. Hunter is loud and boisterous. He'll jump on you the second you walk in the door and claim you as his best friend forever. Riley is quieter, more interested in coloring, singing, or snuggling on the couch. At the time of this writing, my twins are five.

I never really talked about my fears for Riley until this year when the choice to sweep it under the rug was taken away from me. I know lots of three- and four-year-old boys who like to occasionally stomp around in high heels and makeup. But, Riley seemed to love it more than what felt normal for a boy. While Hunter eventually turned to *Star Wars* and *Iron Man,* Riley fell in love with *Tinker Bell* and *The Little Mermaid.* He put towels on his head to give the illusion of hair and wrapped blankets around his body like dresses. He drew pictures of himself in a dress with hair flowing to the floor "like a princess."

About a year ago, the issue went from being an occasional concern to a full-blown emergency. While my husband seemed to be deep in a cave of denial, I was concerned by the more frequent requests for feminine items and behaviors. Riley had requested a dress, and after long talks with my husband, who was still convinced that this was a phase, I spent a long and painful afternoon searching for a dress for my son. It was a bittersweet moment watching him twirl around in complete happiness—something I'd rarely seen in him.

After that, Riley began to ask me when he'd get to be a girl. He asked me every day. And every day I'd tell him that he had a penis so that made him a boy. I was really upset by his questions because I didn't understand why he was so confused about being a girl. Finally, after many months, he stopped.

Several months later, it started again. Only this time, he would just talk about how he couldn't wait to grow up and be a mommy and have a baby in his tummy. Or he'd talk about how pretty his hair would look when it was long like mine. One afternoon, both the kids and I were talking about growing up and Hunter was giggling about having hair on his face like a daddy. Riley again started talking about growing up to be a mommy and I again started correcting him saying, "Riley, you have a penis. You are a boy. You won't grow up to be a mommy; you'll grow up to be a daddy."

Riley got very quiet and said, "I don't want my penis. I wish it would go away so I could have a 'gina like a girl.'" The moment will be forever burned into my memory. I could hear how sad he was, and it was a slap across my face signaling that something was very wrong. I had assumed that maybe he was going to grow up to be gay, but I don't know any gay man who doesn't love his penis.

I began doing internet searches on ridiculous things like "my son wants to wear dresses," and that's when I learned about gender-variant behavior in children. I sat at the computer for hours and just cried and cried because I knew I was reading about my son. My mind immediately jumped to all the scary stories of kids being bullied in junior high and high schools and I was sick with terror for the future of my child.

As the days followed, I searched for a therapist and tried to allow Riley some freedom of expression. He wore a pink sparkly top with camouflage pants, and my husband and I explained that not all boys have to like football and *Star Wars*. Riley could be a boy who liked pink things and dresses and that was okay. For a short time, that worked. Riley was okay with wearing his dress around the house and the pink top outside to play. But, soon, he began begging for more girls' clothes and started telling the neighborhood children that his name was Lisa and that he was really a girl.

I was embarrassed and confused, but also wracked with concern over my child and his twin. We searched for a therapist who had experience working with children like Riley and eventually found one six hours away. In the meantime, I explained to our very concerned babysitter that we had gotten a therapist involved and asked her not to say anything to Riley about his interest in being a girl. I was terrified that she was going to report us to Children's Protective Services for child abuse.

About a week before our trip to see the therapist everything fell apart. Some older kids had teased Riley at the babysitter's house for wearing girls' clothes, and the babysitter told him he could only *pretend* to be a girl. Riley spent hours that night sobbing and begging me to take him to the doctor so she could change his penis into a vagina. He didn't want to pretend to be a girl, he wanted to *be* a girl.

That night, as I held my crying child, I'd have done anything to change his penis into a vagina. I could give him dresses and headbands, but I couldn't give him a girl's body. I was devastated. I didn't know what to do or how to help.

My husband and I called off work the next day just because Riley was so upset. We tried to have a fun family day to distract him, but even on this outing, a child told Riley that a doctor could cut his penis off with a knife or with scissors. Suddenly, we were hiding all the sharp objects in our home. That week was my husband's wake-up call that Riley's behavior was not a phase. We sat crying on the couch one afternoon and made the decision that we would do whatever it took to raise a happy and healthy child.

I placed a frantic call to the therapist who offered to meet with us the next day if we couldn't get Riley calmed down. She suggested girls' panties so that he could put the offending body part in something pretty and feminine. I ran to the store and bought sparkly *Tinker Bell* panties and a little girl's nightgown. We sat down with Riley that night and had a serious talk about not hurting our bodies and let him know that we loved him no matter if he was a girl or a boy.

Despite repeating what I already knew, the therapist gave me a lot of comfort. She said that Riley was extremely gender variant and had a lot of distress over having a penis. I was relieved that we had some answers, but completely over-whelmed by the uncertainty of the future. We were taking things day-by-day and allowing Riley the choice between girls' clothes and boys' clothes.

Over the next few weeks, Riley was adamant that he was not a boy who liked dresses but rather a girl in a boy's body. He would ask me why I didn't say "she" when I talked about him. He got very angry and would yell, "I am *not* a boy!" After several weeks, we decided to go ahead and change to female pronouns.

It was hard. I felt a huge sense of loss for the child that I'd once known. This child, while wonderful and exuberant, and happy beyond anything I'd ever seen before, was not the son I'd always known. I was grieving the loss of my son while watching this happy confident new child emerge.

I was also overwhelmed by guilt. I asked this emerging child what she wanted for her birthday, clarifying that she could ask for boys' toys or girls' toys. This child, who could never tell me any toy that she wanted, suddenly had a list a mile long. I felt horrible that I'd never bothered to take her down the aisles of pink and purple. I never would have said my child had been unhappy until I saw who she was becoming.

This new child was so happy and so alive. I was sick with myself for all those conversations when I told her she was a boy and she would never be a girl. But, at the same time, I would get so embarrassed and almost angry with Hunter when he asked to wear girls' clothes outside, too. It was a difficult transition for our whole family as one son watched his identical twin brother turn into a girl. Desperate to maintain their identity as twins, both children would try out being a girl and I would mute my freaked-out inner voice and give a big smile to my two little boys running around in the backyard wearing girls' bathing suits.

It took Hunter about six months before the reality of having a sister really hit him and he cried about missing his brother. He still has moments where he will come to me crying about missing his brother, but always tells me how much he loves his sister. Every once in a while, usually when Hunter needs to feel closer to his twin, he will decide to "play girl" for the day, although he has stopped asking to borrow Riley's clothes and is content to be a girl-boy in name only. We are supportive of this need to connect with his identical twin and maintain that both our children are wonderful however they identify. It's been quite a process.

I have always considered myself to be open-minded, but I'll be the first to tell you that I didn't even know what the *T* in LGBT stood for. Now, suddenly, I find myself advocating for the rights of all girls and boys to express themselves. I've had to retrain my brain to think beyond male and female and to understand that gender is fluid and not as easy to define for some. This isn't something that I've chosen for my child, but I *have* chosen to believe and support her feelings and identity. I've lost relationships with a few people, but most parents have told me that I'm doing the right thing. I appreciate the comments, but I only have to look at my child's happiness to know this is the right path.

I don't know what the future holds. Riley may one day identify again as a boy, or maybe someday we'll be paying for hormones and sexual reassignment surgery. The most important piece to remember is that my job is to raise my children to be healthy, happy, productive members of society.

I've always told my children that they can be whatever they want to be when they grow up, never knowing how much that would be tested. I can't protect either of them from the struggles they'll face growing up, but I know that they'll be better prepared to handle those difficulties knowing they are loved and accepted for exactly who they are.

Melissa McLaren is an intensive care nurse who is studying for her doctorate with the goal of becoming a nurse practitioner. She is a married mom of twins who lives in the Twin Cities. She spends her free time (if any) running and reading food blogs.

My Name is Alba

Alba Nubia Lopez Gomez

My name is Alba. I am a Latino woman, a lesbian, and a mother of two. I am from Nicaragua, and immigrated to Canada in October of 1988. I have two children, Mateo and Ruben. Mateo is twenty-five years old and Ruben is twenty-one years old. My eldest son Mateo is transgender. On January 1, 2008, Mateo informed me that he was transgender and that he was going to transition.

Mateo has identified as a lesbian since the age of fourteen. When Mateo came out as a lesbian, it was a bit of a shock to me. I was afraid that he was saying that he was a lesbian *because* of me. So, to obtain some clarity on the matter, I sent him for therapy. He let me know that he had always known he was a lesbian. For the most part, I was accepting of it. The fact that

Mateo was a lesbian was not an issue for me or his brother Ruben. I was only concerned about the homophobia that he might encounter. I told family and friends about Mateo's coming out and they embraced Mateo as a young lesbian.

Mateo and his partner Leanne came over to spend New Year's with Ruben and me. Mateo had been in a relationship with Leanne for about two years when he informed me that he was transgender. Mateo's disclosure came as a total shock to me. For a minute, after he told me he didn't feel like a woman and he needed to transition, everything became foggy for me. I could see his mouth moving but I could not hear any sound coming out of it. I felt as if I had fallen into a dark, black hole. My whole life, or what I thought my life to be, had been shaken by his disclosure. I felt a combination of feelings—mostly fear. A thousand questions crossed my mind. I literally felt as if my heart had fallen into the floor and there I was standing not knowing how to put it back into my chest. I tried to recover as fast as I could. I knew that telling me wasn't easy for Mateo, so I had to recover as fast as I could so I could give him some reassurance after such an important disclosure.

I asked him a number of questions: How long had he been feeling like this? What was he planning on doing about this? And, why hadn't he told me before? I also asked him if he was sure about transitioning. I stopped asking more questions because I was too afraid. Mateo said, "You have always said I was the woman you always wanted to be," which I knew meant that he had come out early as gay and never felt any guilt about it. He continued, "I know how hard this must be for you to hear, but I am not that woman! I will always honor the time I have lived as a woman, but I am not that woman; I am not a woman."

At the time, this was all so confusing. I could not put all this information together. Mateo told me that he knew how difficult all this could be for me, and that if I didn't want to see him anymore he would understand. He said he would call a taxi, and I would never have to see him again.

After he said that, I told him that there were two things for me that will never change: the fact that I was his mother and that he was my child, and that I loved him no matter what. We were stuck with each other for life. We were a family. Then I asked him if he could please let me be a part of this whole new process that he was about to start—his transition. I think I may have said that impulsively in order not to lose him, but over time this changed. I also asked him to promise that he would follow all the right steps in order to ensure that his transitioning would be healthy and safe. Mateo agreed on letting me be a part of the transition process. I told him that I would be honored.

Back in 1997, I was doing my second practicum for a Bachelor's degree in Social Work at the "The Living Room," the Village Clinic's drop-in center for people with HIV. There I met and worked with several transgender women, and their stories were very sad. They had no family to comfort them, to help them, to protect them, to support them. Most of them worked in the sex trade as their only means of survival. All of them had to buy females hormones on the black market since there were no doctors who would see them. These thoughts came to mind when Mateo told me about being transgender. The fear of not finding a doctor who could treat him, and the lack of resources—all that came to mind immediately.

I cried a great deal over the next couple of days, as if someone had died. I was very confused, afraid, and angry.

I secretly hoped that this was just a phase for Mateo, and wondered if he would came to his senses and tell me that he wasn't transgender. Then my life could go back to the way it was. It was so confusing, so difficult to understand, and I felt very lonely. My fears took over me.

There was also some guilt. In the midst of all this, I wondered if my being a lesbian had something to do with Mateo being transgender. I also suspected that people would blame Mateo being transgender on my lesbianism and the fact that he grew up in a lesbian household. I also kept asking myself how it was that I never suspected. How come I never saw it? How come I didn't know? How did all these years go by without my seeing his confusion or suffering?

I decided to ask Mateo these questions. He answered, "Because when I said I did not want to wear dresses anymore at the age of four, you said Ok! No more dresses! When I said I did not want to have long hair anymore you let me cut it. I never struggled with clothes because you always let me choose what I wanted to wear." Then he said he never had to struggle like other people with gender roles at home. This seemed true to me. I understood what Mateo was saying, but it did not make me feel any better. I thought that if I had known sooner, I could have done something to make it easier on him.

I still had so many fears. I was afraid of the possible side-effects of taking hormones. The medical aspects of the transition were very scary to me. So I educated myself about transgender issues, and began reading testimonies from other parents whose children were transgender. Reading as much as I could about all the expected changes for him helped ease my fears, but they didn't disappear.

My biggest concern was for Mateo's safety and the cruelty he might encounter. As a lesbian, I knew too well the hate some people have for people like us, people different than the norm. I have survived some homophobia, but I knew that what Mateo was about to face was more complicated and probably more difficult. The fear that this world wasn't ready for someone like Mateo was unshakable. I feared that his relationship would end, that he would not find someone to love him, and that he might end up all alone in life. The fear that no one would recognize how artistic, gentle, loving, caring, and intelligent he is, was enormous. I was completely devastated. My life had taken a turn and I didn't know how to move on. The only thing I was clear about was my love for Mateo, and that I would try to help him, encourage him, protect him, and support him. The love for my child was my only compass and guide. Otherwise, I would have been completely lost, sad, isolated, lonely, guilty, and confused.

I would cry without warning. If I was walking and saw a pregnant woman, I burst into tears. I remember reading *The Sum of Our Days* by Isabel Allende, which is about the importance of families sticking together, and crying through most of the book. This was in some ways comforting and healing for me. I began to realize that my sadness was overwhelming. I decided to go see a psychiatrist who spoke Spanish, an Argentinean woman. I had hope that I would be able to talk to her, and that she would be able to help me through all of this without having to burden Mateo with my pain and insecurities.

The psychiatrist had never treated a transgender person or one of their family members. But at least she was able to understand the cultural part, the difficulties I was facing about coming to terms with it and the pressures that this brought. I was so worried about how to tell my family back home. I didn't want Mateo to feel that he was causing me any kind of pain. Even in the worst moments, I knew he wasn't doing this *to* me. I understood that transitioning was something that he needed to feel complete and whole.

As a lesbian, I know how important it is to live your life in a way that makes you feel complete. I took on a huge risk when I came out as a lesbian to my Latino community, to my coworkers, and to the teachers and administrators at my children's schools. Simply raising two children in a lesbian household in the early nineties was controversial. I was so clear that being out was the only way to live my life, that to stay in the closet would have equaled death to me. So I had a glimpse of how Mateo might feel about becoming the man he needed to be.

I had to take a four-month leave of absence from my job. It was too difficult for me to work, to concentrate. I was still so emotional that I would burst into tears at any time and anywhere. Losing my daughter still seemed unbearable. But taking the time off was necessary and allowed me the time to read and educate myself about transgender issues. I also needed time to integrate everything that was happening to us as a family.

During this period, I would feel guilty because Ruben was not getting the same amount of attention as Mateo. But when I told Ruben that I felt guilty, he always told me not to worry, that he was fine. The few times that Ruben found me crying in the kitchen or heard me crying in the shower, he told me that I should be proud that Mateo was doing what he needed to live his life fully.

Around this time, I found an online group for parents of transgender children. I wrote a brief biography and I waited for admission to the group. Being part of that group saved my life. The sense of being understood made a world of difference to me. The group also gave me something that was very important: it gave me back my hope, hope that Mateo would transition and that he would have a happy, complete, and productive life.

The group also helped me figure out how and when I would tell the rest of my family back in Nicaragua about Mateo's transition. That was a huge concern for me. My parents still weren't dealing very well with the fact that I was a lesbian. I couldn't imagine how they would receive my information about Mateo. I was raised in the Catholic Church, which is not very progressive, so I was really worried about telling my family. Homosexuality was one thing. Transgender issues are a totally different ball game, and there is very little information about it published in Spanish.

I told my parents about Mateo's transition a year ago and I told the rest of my family about four months ago. I don't know how much of my information they understood and how much they have been able to process. What I know is that all of them have expressed their love for my child, and that is all that matters to me.

Last summer Mateo had "top" surgery. He is doing very well, and he and Leanne remain a couple. I have never seen him so happy, so complete, and so confidant.

Through this journey I have met many wonderful, caring, open-minded people. In turn, they have helped me push myself to be more open-minded, more caring, and more aware of the differences among the people we encounter in our lives. I even coordinate, with another mother, a group for parents of transgender children in my city.

This has all been an incredible experience, and quite a ride! I no longer have a daughter but I have a wonderful, happy, intelligent, compassionate son whom I admire, respect, and love more than life itself.

Alba Nubia Lopez Gomez is a forty-five-year-old Latino lesbian from Nicaragua. She lives with her youngest son Ruben in Winnipeg, Manitoba, Canada.

One of Life's Surprises

Brenda Lee

I was an only child and was raised on a farm in Eastern Oregon. I attended a one-room country schoolhouse. During the Depression years we had to move to the nearest town nearly twenty miles away, where I would attend junior high and high school. I graduated from high school when I was sixteen, and I immediately began to work in a law office.

I married one of the boys from my high school, and although the marriage was not the happiest, it produced two wonderful sons. Our family of four was complete as far as I was concerned. I had secretly hoped that one of my children would be a girl, but when my husband suggested we have another child, I said no. Little did I know I already had one!

I never became a grandmother. My younger son married

a couple of times, but there were never any children. My older son once brought home what I thought was a serious girl friend, but he never married, and now I understand why. I always told my sons that as long as they were happy, so was I.

A month after I retired, I was living in Oregon, and I received an email from my eldest child. Here is what the email said:

"Mom: I'm sending you a letter in the mail that you should get Friday or maybe Saturday. It has to do with something I need to tell you.

No, I'm not dying—at least I don't think I am.

It is something important, so I want you to read this before we talk. This is the best way I could think of to tell you. I know it will be a surprise but don't worry about anything because I'm okay. All my love…"

And, of course, the first thing I did was get on the phone and call him. I had to ask if he was okay. I asked why he couldn't just tell me now. But he just said wait and read the letter. And then I called my other son and told him about the email and said I was worried and asked if he knew anything. What did he think was going on? But he just said, "Don't worry Mother, I am sure everything will be okay, just wait until you get the letter." But until the letter arrived, worry I did.

Thank goodness my younger son and his wife arrived for a visit before the letter did. It arrived in a large envelope, which surely contained more than just the letter I had been awaiting! I opened it, dropping out a small manila envelope as I did so, but I didn't look at that until much later. I began to read the letter and the tears began. Even now, as I reread this letter a few years later to type some of it into my story, the tears are coming.

"Dear Mom," the letter began, "First of all, I need to say that this is something I need to do and this is the best way I could come up with. I sense that you know there is something different about how I have been feeling lately although I've actually always felt this way. It's just that now is the time for me to do what I have to do.

"I have been seeing a therapist for nearly a year now. To be simple about it, all my life I have wished, felt and wanted to be female. Not being able to be my true self has caused me a great deal of pain and heartache. I know I covered it well from everyone. Even today I doubt anyone would suspect how I really feel.

"In basic terms, I am transsexual, or gender-dysphoric as it's termed by psychologists. When I was little I was so scared that someone would find out. I truly believed that I was the only one in the world and thought I must be nuts. I dreamed every night that I was changed into a girl. I prayed and I cried to no avail. I imagined and tried to think of all kinds of ways to make it come true.

"I remember feeling this way from the first time I could think. I knew something was wrong but couldn't figure it out except that my mind kept telling me I wasn't supposed to be like this. Until I read about Christine Jorgensen I had no idea that you could change your gender.

"In order to hide my true feelings I did lots of things boys did to try and be one of them. This is a common theme that we try to be as masculine as we can in hopes that it will go away. It never does. Some of us can't stand it and suicide is often the result. Others like me find ways to suppress our feelings most of our lives until we just can't take it anymore.

"I confess I would wear your clothes on several occasions when I was young until I outgrew them. I was sure you knew but you never said anything. Wearing the clothes did make me feel good for the moment but it wasn't what I wanted. I so desperately wanted to be female, and though I could hide it from the world I couldn't hide it from myself.

"College was a difficult time too. Some of these things you probably don't know, but I did an awful lot of drinking and drugs in college. I didn't realize then what I was doing but I know now I was only suppressing my feelings. I'm sure even growing the beard was another attempt to hide and try to feel more masculine. Believe me, it didn't work at all.

"In order to correct things I started therapy with a specialist in this area. I started to take female hormones in April of this year. The hormones have changed me somewhat and will continue to do so. I have done laser hair removal and I am starting electrolysis. You may or may not notice some of the changes but they will become more noticeable as time goes on.

"I plan to begin living as a woman full-time shortly after I retire if everything works out.

"I know this may leave you in shock because I know it would shock me to find that the son I knew felt like someone else. I know that you may have lots of questions. Hopefully some of the information in the envelope will help to answer many of them.

"I know you have always said you would love me no matter what. I guess I'm putting that to the test. I do know that I love you regardless of whether or not you are able to accept me.

"I also want you to know that you have always been the woman I most admired in my life and you have always been a source of inspiration to me in so many ways. I may not have found ways to tell you that before.

"I love you with all my heart."

I'm not sure when the tears stopped or how long it took before I could speak. I know I passed the letter to my husband to read and my son came over and gave me a big hug and said, "Everything will be okay."

I wasn't too sure about that. I had many thoughts of how my child would be accepted by my second husband, who had known her for twenty years and enjoyed her as my son. I also worried about how all our other relatives would take this. Then there was the fact that she worked in a very male-dominated industry, and I was afraid they would not accept her. And what about all her friends and the girl she had dated earlier? I was afraid for her and couldn't stop the negative thoughts and questions.

But my other son was right. Everything is now okay in many ways which I wouldn't have imagined back then. In fact, I have that daughter I always secretly wanted, but it took a while for it all to seem real. That day, it was my turn to compose myself and make the phone call and let my new daughter know how much I loved her—no matter what. The first words out of my mouth as the tears came were something like "I got your letter and I will always love you." She was crying as well and neither one of us could say much. Our conversation mostly consisted of repeating "I love you" and shedding many tears. She said she would be over to visit soon, and she asked me to please read the brochures she sent, because she hoped they would help me understand. And they did.

My husband made me sit down every day and talk to him

about my daughter and what had happened and how I was feeling, and he encouraged me to seek outside help. My son called frequently to see if I was okay and talk about his new sister. The love they had always shared was still there and that made me feel good. There was a family gathering with nieces and nephews, and my new daughter was accepted by everyone. I read the brochures and called various people, and I was able to meet a couple of ladies who had themselves transitioned some years earlier. This gave me lots of insight into the whole process. I also joined PFLAG where I met a woman with a son who had transitioned, and we have become close friends, still visiting over coffee and lunch several times a month. I believe that over these past six years, I, too, have made a complete transition—from having a son to having a daughter. No longer do I find myself thinking *he* and *him*. I am not sure I could have made it without the love and support of my husband, my son and his wife, my close friends and nieces and nephews, and, above all, without the love of my daughter.

So here I am enjoying my daughter who moved to our same town two-and-a-half years ago. We see each other at least once a week, sometimes twice, and we have even made some trips together. We have a wonderful and continuing mother/daughter relationship. She is playing lots of golf and volunteering at a local performing arts center. She is happier than I have ever seen her and enjoying her new life.

All I can recommend to mothers who find out they have a transgender child is to believe them, trust them, support them, and, whatever you do, love them.

Brenda Lee is a mother living in Oregon. She is retired and enjoys spending time with her family, including her wonderful new daughter.

A Blessing in Disguise

Judy Sennesh

In retrospect, I have no idea why I was drawn to buy and devour Amy Bloom's beautiful collection of short stories, *A Blind Man Can See How Much I Love You*. Not only did I buy it; but I also sent E. a copy at school, telling her how wonderful it was. This was several years before my child announced she was transgender.

The very first story in the book is about a mother accompanying her child for sexual reassignment surgery. That story still brings tears to my eyes because it's all about the power of unconditional love for our children.

E. started the conversation about being transgender by leaving her copy of the very same book on my bed with a Post-It saying, "This is about me, except for the bottom surgery. We need to talk."

Truth be told, I had been dreading this announcement for about two years. Historically, E. had communicated things about herself, and her life, by talking about people other than herself. I imagine it was a way of testing the waters, of seeing how I reacted before she spilled the real beans all over the floor. I had been hearing a lot about a particular girl at school, who was one of her teammates on the rugby team. People didn't seem to care for her very much because she was living as a male and "transitioning." I don't remember if I'd ever heard that word before.

Prior to the big announcement, we'd been through a very unpleasant experience with my older son's future in-laws. E. was told that she couldn't be in the wedding party unless she wore a dress, something she hadn't done since her bat mitzvah, and so she wasn't in the wedding party. She withdrew from the harmful conflict with the announcement: "I hate big weddings, anyway." But in order to support her as best we could, we bought her a navy blue suit, a white silk shirt, and a yellow necktie, which she wore to the wedding. The in-laws weren't thrilled, but I was very proud.

When E. finally told me about her decision, she'd been doing research for a long time and came to me with a plan in place. This plan included taking off her fall semester to visit friends studying overseas. She had already selected a surgeon for her "top" surgery and had a January appointment tentatively booked at a hospital outside of Chicago. She also informed me that I was *not* coming along on the surgery trip—a very wise move on my wise kid's part. A wonderful friend was going with her and that was that. In a way, after watching her spend the whole, hot summer binding her chest and wearing layer upon layer of clothing to hide substantial breasts, I couldn't wait for it all to be done. I was quite fortunate, and so glad, to have such a smart and proactive kid.

We were very lucky to have that summer pretty much to ourselves. I asked all the questions other mothers ask, especially, *"Why* can't you just be a butch lesbian and forget all this medical stuff?"* She explained that gender wasn't the same as sexual orientation: gender is about who you *know* you are and orientation is about the people you're attracted to. I listened and didn't quite understand, but I made like I did and headed for the Internet. I was calm, in fact, I was so calm that she kept telling me I had to find a shrink because I couldn't possibly be so OK.

But actually, the more I read, and the more people I reached out to, the better I felt. And suddenly her past behavior started to make sense. My very smart kid had been having a hard time at school, had been experiencing insomnia, and had been put on mood-stabilizing medication. It was frightening for me to see my formerly focused, outgoing child hide in her bedroom and become more sullen as the days passed. I was the mommy and here was something I couldn't fix—the ultimate failure for a Jewish mother. Could this be what that was all about? Was this the reason she would occasionally tell me she was "different" than other people in our family while she was growing up, but would never explain why? And, was this why she had come to me at least three times when she was much younger to ask if she could change her name, and the new, proposed names were all gender-neutral, like Pat, Lee, or Ricky? Who would have ever guessed that these were attempts to tell me that she was, in her brain and heart, my son and not my daughter? At the time, it was too far off my radar to even be considered as a possibility.

She told me about the TransKidsFamily website and I joined. Dave Parker, bless his heart, a member of the list-serv and then President of PFLAG-TNET introduced me to the woman who was the NYC Trans-Coordinator and we spoke on the phone. She was terrific, and sane, and "normal," which was extremely comforting. I devoured information from any source I could find. I read Jamison Green's terrific book, *Becoming a Visible Man,* and his handsome author photo became my psychic friend.

Looming ahead were the hardest days I was to experience: E.'s time abroad traveling though Europe. It is ironic that my totally androgynous child, who had been periodically buzzing her hair for years, would now be one of the few people on earth with an exquisite passport photo. I don't mean "nice" or "lovely," I truly mean exquisite. With short curly hair, big blue eyes, and full beautiful lips, it was a passport photo anyone would kill to have. And here she was, heading for a trip where she would be going through airport security many times, looking very much like a young man. I was almost brought to my knees with terror in those post-9/11 days when having proper identification was the watchword of everyone's faith. Would she get pulled out of line and interrogated? Humiliated? God forbid, strip-searched?

These were the days I didn't sleep every time I knew she was flying from one city to another. And in the end what happened was...nothing—not a question, not an embarrassment. She was always treated properly and no differently than anyone else. With all the awful stories we hear about gay bashings, and with Matthew Shepard still fresh in the minds of the gay community and their allies, the relief when E. came home was overwhelming—the sigh heard around my world.

As that fall drew to an end, there was a consultation with the surgeon on the calendar, which was combined with a trip to visit friends at school. E. came home excited about the surgery and with very positive feelings about the surgeon and his staff. When that date finally arrived, I sat by the phone all day, thinking about every cut, scrape, and bloody injury that my child had ever suffered. I was unable to bear the thought that someone was removing parts of her body, and afraid that she would be in pain and suffer. And so, it came as a welcome surprise when we spoke that night, and through a slightly medicated haze she said to me, "I feel great, and thank God they're gone!" It was an important turning point for both of us. I never looked back.

The surgery healed well and quite quickly, and three months later testosterone injections began. We filed for a legal name change for E. at the urging of an attorney friend who said he would step in if we needed him. We didn't, and it was quick and fairly painless. With each new, corrected piece of identification, I rejoiced because I felt my kid was becoming safer and safer in a strange world full of uncharted territory.

The great disappointment was (and continues to be) that we couldn't get a corrected New York City birth certificate. The City had been on the verge of changing its guidelines for transgender people, then backed off at the very last moment— a fight that continues to be waged. And the most exciting moment came when a new US passport arrived by Priority Mail, with his new, legal name, indicating that E. was male.

There had been one, interim request from the Passport Agency asking for a letter from E.'s surgeon, which the doctor quickly supplied.

I remember thinking of the scene in *Miracle on 34th Street* when all the letters for Santa Claus are delivered to the court-house where Kris Kringle is on trial. "If the US Passport Agency says my kid is male," I thought to myself, "that better be good enough for everyone else."

And so, E., who had become a "he" along the way, causing us to grapple with the dreaded pronoun problem, graduated from college with his correct name on his diploma, and with his extended posse of friends fully intact. He stayed with the terrific young woman he'd met senior year of college (when it looked like they were both lesbians), and then got a job as a high school teacher. They were married last summer in a wedding so filled with joy that you can feel the happiness pouring out of the photos.

Unlike many parents who, with good reason, mourn the loss of their son or daughter when they transition, I've never been to that place. There was a brief time when I felt like my child was slipping away from me, going through something I didn't understand and couldn't help with. That was terrifying. But I remember the first time someone asked me if I had children and I was able to answer, "Yes, I have two wonderful sons." How very special that felt!

I believe that transgender people suffer from something akin to a birth defect (although I don't like the word "defect"), and we made a correction. As with many transgender kids, once the corrections are even begun, the insomnia, depression, and other emotional problems start to disappear. I didn't lose my daughter; I got back my smart, resourceful, and caring child, in a very slightly altered form. I couldn't be happier, or more grateful.

Judy Sennesh is the very proud mother of two wonderful sons and their wives. She has been a real estate professional in New York City for many years. She sits on the Board of Directors of PFLAG NYC, and facilitates two support groups, one of which is for parents with transgender children.

I Wish Her Happiness Most of All

Dana Lane

I was born an only child in Los Angeles, with both parents living in the home. I was raised as a Lutheran but converted to the Baptist faith once I got married. I am still married to the father of all of my children, and we have been together for twenty-seven years. We have four children: De'Nina is the oldest at twenty-five years of age, Ricky Jr. is our twenty-two-year-old son, Daija is our nineteen-year-old daughter, and Darrah, who is our fourteen-year-old daughter. I currently reside in St. Louis with my husband and our two youngest children.

Our parenting style is simple. We go to school and work Monday through Friday, and go to church on Sunday. As Baptists we believe that marriage is a union between a man and a woman—and nothing more. As a parent I expect good grades and proper behavior from my children, in public and at home. My preconceived ideas about parenting, especially when the children were young, included that girls should wear dresses with lace socks, neatly combed hair with bows and barrettes, and maybe attend a dance class on the weekend. Boys were to wear jeans, keep their hair combed or cut short, and play sports.

I began to think something was different with our eldest child, De'Nina, when I realized that she had never dated. All of her friends in high school were mostly tomboys on the basketball team, or were guys on the basketball court. When I asked her about her sexual preference, she replied that she was "asexual," but I wasn't sure what she meant by that. She attended the same school as her cousin who didn't associate with her there at all. I felt that Nina was withdrawn, preferring online classes instead of school with other students. She also seemed uncomfortable at times around us, her parents, as well as around other family members.

Nina first mentioned a year ago that she was taking male hormone shots, and my first concerns were whether the shots would agree with her system. What would happen to her in five years? Would she become chemically imbalanced, have organ failure, or even grow another arm with extra fingers? I was really worried and asked her to stop.

The conversation never came up again, so I was unaware of the path she took from there. Around her birthday this year, she expressed that she wanted to change her name to De'Nier. Once again, I asked her if she was sure she wanted to do this. I knew from what I had been told that this was a common step right before people change their sex, so I asked her to think about it.

I can't really say I've come to peace with my child's

transition. She is still in the middle of it, and I am still hoping she changes her mind about this. My two youngest daughters have accepted the fact that she is what she is. However, my son has mentioned to me that he feels she will never be a man like he is. I try my best not to mention too much about Nina's transition to my husband, but my daughter has told him about her name change, and he told her to do what makes her happy. Neither my child nor I have discussed telling my husband all the details of the planned transition.

As a parent, the hardest thing to accept or understand about this journey is whether we did something wrong in raising our child. Should I have sent her to another school? Dressed her differently? Avoided sports or made her hang around different children? Overall, I'm proud of Nina. She is not on drugs, has a level head, tries hard to keep a job, and clearly wants better for herself.

Although it is difficult, I've learned to trust God and not worry about the process. As a result, my relationship with my child is getting better. I am able to talk to her about some issues and give my opinion without her getting upset. My hope for the future is for me and my child to remain close. I would like for her to be able to come to me and talk if need be. I hope she succeeds in her quest to be comfortable in her own skin. And, most of all, I wish her happiness.

Dana Lane is an African American middle-class citizen. She runs her own professional medical staffing company in St. Louis, Missouri, and hopes to expand her business nationwide within a few years.

Hatch! Mister Sister

Mary Doyle

Adapted from the zine Hatch! Mister Sister, *originally published in 2006*

It's a cold February morning and the yard is full of crows, *caw-cawing.* I've been in labor over fifty-one hours; my belly so full of baby. I am ready for the end.

Who on earth is this kid inside of me? Soon enough I will know. Twenty minutes later, I'm holding a naked wet baby and hearing myself say "Oh good lord, it's ALIVE!" Giving birth is pretty amazing. Here I was with this little creature in my arms, pink and perfect, those big eyes looking up at me for the first time, both of us full of wonder, and with such different perspectives. What have I gotten myself into? Little did I know.

I'd been certain I was pregnant with a boy, so my surprise was great when I saw her.

"Well, so much for mother's intuition," I joked. I didn't have a girls' name picked out, but three days later, I was the proud young mother of my little Helen.

Life with baby crept along. I started midwifery school later that year with Helen in tow. I did the attachment parenting thing—family bed, sling, nursing 'til she could say "I want booby right *now* mother, please." We moved around a lot in those first couple of years—an internship in Jamaica, a rainbow gathering, a tipi on an organic garlic farm in Montana, a cabin in the woods of upstate New York—but Chicago has always been home base.

There is a story that has become a bit of personal Helen/Asher folklore. He asks me to tell it every chance we get, so I'll share it here with you.

It's Helen's first birthday. My aunt had given her the most beautiful party dress, and I'd been saving it for just this day. It is white with puffy sleeves and pastel embroidered flowers, a gathered waist, and a lacy collar—so lovely! I'm bragging shamelessly to our party guests, and when I'm done with that, I pick up the phone, call my best friend and begin to describe my beautiful, amazing, sweet, intelligent, charming, genius one-year-old in her adorable birthday party dress.

Well, meanwhile, Helen decides she's had quite enough of this shameless display. She is sitting in her bouncy chair playing with her toes and trying to figure out how the heck she is going to get out of this dreadful dress. Then she spots them. Across the room, in a heap of wrapping paper, scotch tape, and bows lay the perfect tools for her salvation. She unbuckles the strap on her bouncy seat, climbs out and begins creepy crawling toward her destination.

I am too busy bragging to notice her slow turtle trek across the kitchen. By the time I do look down, it is too late. Helen is sitting on the floor, beaming mischievously, holding a large pair of scissors in her chubby hands and calmly opening and closing, opening and closing the blades. The beautiful party dress has been cut to shreds. I let out a horrified yelp. Little Helen just looks up at me with a satisfied grin, delighted with her handiwork.

Years later, when Helen was three, she began taking various boys names. First it was "Blake," then "Jack," then "*Mighty* Jack" (and if you left out the "Mighty" you'd certainly be corrected). She also tried on "Brandon," "Henry," "Vinny," and several others.

One evening while she was in the tub, she asked me, "Mom, when is my penis going to grow in?" This was the first of many such questions that I had no idea how to answer. Nor did Dr. Spock or those Sears people. I stuttered through my first attempt to explain the physical differences between boys and girls, keeping it as simple as possible.

She was not satisfied with my answer, but at least a conversation had begun. It would be put on the shelf for a month or two, but never dropped. Over the next couple of years, she became more and more assertive about expressing her male gender. She never talked about wanting to be a boy, and never discussed what she would be someday, but rather: "Mom, I'm really a boy."

At first, he spoke these words only to me, in whispers or at home, being careful not to attract too much attention.

But, bit by bit, he became more bold. By the time he was five years old, he'd correct me in public when I introduced him as my daughter, and began talking about being a boy with other members of my family.

In all honesty, it didn't bother me much that my little girl baby was growing up to be a handsome young lad, but other people did mind—a whole lot, in fact. My family, parents of his school friends, and even my close friends made it a point to tell me quite often how crazy this seemed to them. Of course it was hard not to take this personally. It felt as though the sanity of my supportive stance was being called into question. By the time he was five years old, it had become impossible to continue hiding behind excuses like "it's just a phase," or, "isn't that cute."

By now he had asked me plenty of times to refer to him as my son, buy him briefs, and cut his hair. In hindsight, it was not with his best interest in mind that I resisted. My gut said just let the kid be! Don't interfere with his/her self-expression. I stayed silent because I was afraid of the repercussions of being seen as supportive, or worse, "encouraging."

Eventually, protecting my family, friends and acquaintances from my kid's gender identity was not worth it. I had to choose. I chose to believe him.

Sometime during Helen's Kindergarten, however, I did go on what I call the Girls Rock! Campaign, complete with a Girls Rock! button. I was thinking maybe I could sell her on the tomboy idea and make both of our lives a hell-of-a-lot easier. We played soccer, I bought her a really cool dress at a thrift store that I insisted was a boy/girl dress, and I talked a lot about how girls can do anything they want, and when they grow up, they can be anything they want. We listened to *Free to Be You and Me* all the time, and read lots of fairy tales with powerful women characters. She was on board for a month and a half or so wearing the boy/girl dress and the button, soaking up the stories, and kicking around a soccer ball with me every chance she got.

Then one night, sitting on her bed in her pj's after story time, she said to me in a calm, soft voice, "Hey mom, I know girls rock and everything, but I'm still a boy." I hugged him and said, "OK, I love you just as much."

Now and then I'd still prod a little. Like a year and a half ago, in Portland, we were reading this lovely fairy tale with a warrior woman who was tall, strong, and beautiful, of course. I said, "Look at her. You can grow up to be strong and powerful like her." And Helen replied, "Yes, I know, but I want to grow up to be like him" and pointed to the big fat king beside the warrior princess. My little guy...bless 'im.

For a time, we moved back in with my folks, and my kid started school at the local public elementary school. I went in the day before he started and told the principal that my child, Helen, would be telling all the kids in her class that she was a boy, and that I did not want her to be contradicted. Plus, I said, we'd have to work out the bathroom issue.

The principal was no nonsense about the business of running a school, and he had no interest in making a big issue of this. He asked me what we needed, granted all requests, and sent me on my way. My next stop was the school social worker. The social worker was also very cool about our situation. She met with Helen's new teacher right away, and then they met with the principal and school nurse after that. His teacher decided to wait and see how Helen introduced himself to the class, and not interfere. The students began using male pronouns (to Helen's delight), so the teacher consistently conformed to this pattern.

However, he was still going by Helen, which created confusion when combined with a male pronoun, and drew more attention than he cared for. His classmates would sometimes ask, flat out and in front of others, whether he was a boy or a girl. Perhaps these were innocent and friendly questions, but for Asher it became an issue of dread and shame. He finished the year there, and on the last day the social worker, whom I liked, told me she was going to another school. Bummer. Who knew what next year would bring?

Summer camp was rough. I didn't do much in the way of advocacy or meetings before camp started, and on the first day, we walked up to the counselor, who pulled out a clipboard and said "who's this little guy?" "He's Helen" I replied. The counselor looked back down at his clipboard with a bewildered expression and then said "Oh! Well she's all set." That summer, Helen came to the conclusion that her birth name would have to go. "Mom, they think I'm a girl because I have a girls' name. I need a new name before school starts." We made a list of our favorite boys' and gender-neutral names, and Asher was the lucky winner.

I'm proud of my son for finding the strength to cry when he's hurt, even as he tells me that "boys are not supposed to." And I'm proud of him for having the courage to be himself in a world that tells him it's impossible or forbidden for him to do so.

He makes me laugh too. I feel pretty lucky. Last week we

were setting up a board game in my room after his bath. Out of the blue, he shared this with me: "Mom, I'm not a boy or a girl. I'm a boy and a girl. I can be anything I want, and I can switch someday, too." Moments like this remind me to keep breathing and trust that the kid is all right.

Being human is to judge, again and again, unless and until we unlearn this behavior. Mothers are such a frequent and easy target. As a once very young single mother of a transgender kid, you might imagine I've had more than ample opportunities to be on the receiving end of this. Thus, before I continue, I must ask that you please hang your opinions and "right" answers on the hat hook and put on a pair of my shoes. If you will do this, or at least try, I'll show you around the house of our current reality—one family's navigation into transgender puberty.

Since Asher was five I've been asked: "What will you do when puberty hits?" The best answer I could come up with is: "We'll cross that bridge when we come to it." Meanwhile, I did my best to research our rather limited options. Below is a brief summery of what I discovered.

Option A: Get Lupron, a hormone blocker, injected into his shoulder once a month. This would block his estrogen, thus halting any physical "symptoms" of puberty in their tracks for thirty days, and then do it again the next month, and the next, until starting transition—or not. And then Option B: No Lupron, puberty goes along as you imagine it might, with curves and bumps and blood, *Oh my!*

Depending on who you are and what informs your own beliefs, this may seem at first an obvious and simple choice. I have, however, been blessed with a special knack for being contrary, playing devil's advocate, and seeing both sides of any issue. This has given me ample opportunity to learn about and argue both sides. And, this has left me with a long list of very good questions.

First and foremost, how can I know if Lupron will be safe for his body? The jury's still out on this; our kids are still the guinea pigs, and rumor has it Lupron injections may increase the risk of osteoporosis and cancer of the reproductive organs. But then again, so will cell phones, and living near power plants, and drinking the water.

Then there is the issue of fertility, which Lupron followed by transition will most likely destroy. But, on the other hand, Asher says with certainty that he never wants to be pregnant, he'll adopt if he has kids at all. Still, how can I expect a thirteen-year-old to make such a grown-up decision? I've known several transgender guys who decided at thirty that they wanted to grow a baby and breastfeed, and I imagine many of them felt just like Asher at thirteen. So is it ethical for me to let him make such a grown-up choice at thirteen that will jeopardize his fertility forever?

Next, let's talk about privilege. I'm sure many a graduate school thesis paper has been written on this subject already, but let me try and do it some justice in five short sentences. Lupron is some expensive shit! About $500 per month, and that's for injections, which is the cheaper option. Even if we do find some way to pay for this, what about those who can't? Is passing now a commodity of the wealthy white urban class? How will my kid learn to be an ally to those less privileged if his own privilege depends upon his passing?

And this brings us to the last question: what's the deal with passing anyway? I'm serious, what does that even mean? What exactly is he passing as? A "normal" boy? Even if he succeeds in passing, he is still trans, and he'll always be, so isn't passing just a way of remaining silent and invisible? Oh right, and *safe*—less vulnerable to bullying, harassment, and torturous self-loathing. Yes, we are creatures of our very real environments.

Look at the world we live in! It is still, in many ways, a very hostile place toward transgender people, whether they are "out and proud" or just unsuccessful at passing. What is easier, to change the whole world, or to allow my kid some more ease navigating middle school as a tranny? What about internalized misogyny? As a mother, watching my twelve-year-old suffer the dread and horror of anticipating that first blood is something I can only hear so much of before I ask, "What's the big f'ing deal? Bleeding is an amazing miracle of life and mystery and power and it's a part of who you are!" And then I say, "Get over it!" And he says, "Geez, mom, you are clueless." And I say, "Yes, well that may be and all, but I am here to tell you that bleeding is not the end of your life, it's part of your power!"

What we finally agreed on was that Asher would wait until his first period, and then he'd be able to choose for himself. He could decide what route was best for him, with the guidance of his health care team for at least 12 months. This way, he could experience for himself what this blood business is all about, instead of solely relying on his friend's horror stories. This way, we might honor his passage into adulthood by trusting him with this very adult decision. This way, he might still have the option of growing a baby when he's older, should he desire that. This way, he might look forward to this important transition into adulthood and eagerly await his menarche ritual: his first monthly trip to the clinic!

This process began last October, and he was very excited when the big day came. Asher has an awesome team of health care providers: a wonderful nurse practitioner and a brilliant endocrinologist, both intelligent, caring, and witty women. They have been surprising allies in many ways. On top of it all, Medicaid has thus far paid for his Lupron injections, a pleasant surprise that has made all this possible.

Finally, for everyone else going through this, I must tell you this is no magic bullet! True, the period has come and gone, he passes at school and thus is at less risk of bullying, and most of his classmates are unaware of his transition. There is a lot of stress in keeping this very significant part of his identity a secret. What if he gets outed by a friend? How will he learn to be proud of his authentic other-ness? And, good grief, dating is just wrought with land mines!

Last week I drove Asher to Jacksonville to put him on a plane to Philly for the Trans Health Conference. In the car he told me that he finally understood why I made him wait until he got his period, and he's really glad about it. He said he doesn't have to fear the unknown because he knows now what it feels like, and he wishes all his friends could know, too. So, he said maybe he'll just have to tell them.

Mary Doyle lives in Gainesville, Florida, with her son Asher and cat Eleanor. In addition to single parenting, she spends her time being a student, teaching childbirth classes, being a doula, making art, gardening, practicing yoga, and being contrary.

Jenna, now John

Ingrid Charbonneau

The story of my daughter Jenna, who is now John, was a bit of a surprise to me. And I didn't think that anything would be able to shock me at my age.

Jenna was a tall and beautiful woman, standing at over six feet tall. As a teenager in California, she modeled for a department store in their advertising newspaper supplement. Jenna was the type of woman that turned heads as she walked down the street. I believe this was because of her height, her long dark hair, her brown eyes, and her beautiful olive complexion. Besides her outward physical beauty, she (now he) has a very high IQ, and received a 4.0 average throughout her college years, graduating *summa sum laude*.

Jenna was always compassionate. As a young adult she

worked with people with AIDS, and at one point, even wanted to become a Catholic nun so that she could help others. She also believed that she could help make the Catholic Church more accepting of outsiders such as the lesbian and gay community. When she realized she couldn't counteract the strong dogma of the Catholic Church on her own, she became drawn to the spiritual practice of Buddhism. My child found a niche in Buddhism, and continues to practice this faith.

Jenna didn't do a lot of dating in high school, but never hinted that there was any particular reason for this behavior. After high school, she moved to San Francisco and had a few boyfriends, all of whom did not last very long. I think I attributed this to the fact that she was an independent woman who generally didn't put up with much baloney from men. Eventually, she met an Irishman whom she dated for about four years. She even went on a trip to Ireland with him to meet his family. However, during the trip, there was some strife concerning acceptance of her within their family, and she returned home alone.

After this, she met another man in the Bay Area through a mutual friend. He convinced her to move to his hometown in Oregon, and they lived together for about two years. She became pregnant with a son, who was to become my one and only grandchild. She didn't immediately tell me she was pregnant, but I eventually guessed. This was fairly typical for us, as she was always closely guarded about some aspects of her life. Shortly after her son's birth, Jenna and her partner split up, leaving her alone with a young child. I was only able to see my grandchild for about one week a year, which was not my pref- erence. Jenna lived on her own with her son for five years until

I eventually moved to be closer to them. I was so happy to be there for my grandson's first day of kindergarten!

At this point, there was absolutely no indication in my mind that Jenna was soon to transition. She wore feminine clothing and makeup, and her hair was always long and styled. When we discussed this some years later, my child told me that despite having an outwardly feminine appearance, she had always felt that she should have been a boy.

The conversation about my daughter's transition began around three years ago, when I started to notice pamphlets and books on topics involving gender and transition on her bookshelf. She's a big reader, and we have always enjoyed sharing literature, but these publications were not on the usual topics we shared. However, nothing was said by either of us—yet.

As has been the customary pattern, I was not the first to know about Jenna's forthcoming change. Jenna had already revealed it to her close friends and her sister. A few weeks later, she was finally able to tell me of her decision to transition from female to male. I was shocked, but as is usual for me in times of adversity, I relied on my sense of humor to help me process this surprising news. I said, "Why can't you just be a lesbian?" Jenna looked at me, and said, "Because I'm not." Since then, she has had her breasts removed and has taken hormone therapy. At first the changes came gradually, then her facial hair grew in and the changes became more noticeable. John also has short hair, so that is another big difference from Jenna.

After finding out about this change in my daughter, I shed a lot of tears. For one thing, I could not understand how I was going to tell my family. I worried about all the problems that this change would bring. I was also tremendously upset imagining the effect this would have on my grandson, and I worried about how other people would treat him as a result of her decision. I think about how cruel children, as well as adults, can be. My grandson is now twelve and seems to be coping very well. I still worry that some conflict will come up with his friends, or with his teachers or the other parents when John attends his school functions. I wonder how my grandson introduces his parent? I do know that he chooses to call John a gender-neutral nickname, rather than "Mom" or "Dad."

Over the years, I have tried to be as supportive as I could, but it has been very difficult at times. One thing that has proven hard for me is the use of pronouns. After all, for almost forty years I have referred to my child as *she,* and now I have to say *he.* My child gets very upset when I slip up! I also get uncomfortable when people stare at us in public. Even though my child now presents as quite masculine, I get the sense that sometimes people are trying to figure out what may be different about him.

We recently went through old family pictures and there were some of Jenna as a little girl. I started to cry, and John asked me what was wrong. I told him that it was hard to look at pictures that reminded me of all the changes we had been through, and that those earlier times depicted in the photos had been happy days for me. To see my child, who was such a beautiful woman, transition to being such a masculine looking man, is still very much a shock. And I do miss having my daughter as my daughter.

As far as telling friends and other family members, I have been selective about who knows. I have told some close cousins and my best friends. My mother recently passed away, but was never told. Even though the grandparents were an important and supportive part of Jenna's younger years, her grandfather, my father, has not aged well and has become very judgmental in his older years. There is no way that he could ever accept Jenna's transition. As a result, Jenna, now John, cannot attend any family functions—even my mother's recent funeral. My brothers also do not know yet. They're good guys, but we don't know how they would react. So for now, we are not sharing this news. Jenna's father, from whom I am divorced, also does not know.

To better deal with Jenna's transition, I attended the local PFLAG meetings in my town for about a year. I often felt like I was just going there and crying, or complaining about the changes in my child. There was only one other parent of a transgender child who attended, and even though I liked everyone else there and was made to feel welcome by them, I felt we were on a different journey. Most of the parents were very accepting of their gay and lesbian children, and I felt I was taking away from the joy these parents were experiencing in this acceptance. I remember one day voicing that I would have so much preferred that Jenna be a lesbian and not transgender. At least, I said, she would still be a she and I would not have the daunting experience of trying to remember the correct pronoun for my child. This was not something to which they could relate. I did form a strong friendship with the other parent of an adult transgender child there, and we are friends to this day.

One of the most surprising things about Jenna's transition is that I have found that I can no longer pick my child out of a crowd. Last week I watched John walking down the stairs and it was like looking at my former husband from forty years ago. I am blonde and Swedish, and my ex-husband was Irish and Italian, and both my kids inherited his darker coloring and features. Now, as a man, John could be my husband's twin, they look so much alike!

It has been two years since John's transition. I still have a hard time of it, but am happy to say that I am doing a lot better with everything—except dealing with the old memories and remembering to use the correct pronoun! It is John's life to live in the way he chooses. Thus, he has done the only thing that he could do: live a life true to his feelings and to his nature.

Ingrid Charbonneau is a retired feature writer and historical archivist living in the Pacific Northwest.

Silly Ma Ma! I'm A Boy

Kate Levy

September 2007

In 2007, my husband Micah and I traveled with our oldest daughter Jie Jie, then age five, to China to adopt a three-and-a-half-year-old little girl named Di Di. Jie Jie and Di Di were to be "provincial sisters," that is, adopted from the same province.

October 5, 2007

At 1:00 a.m., we arrived home from China with our child Di Di. Bleary eyed and sleep deprived, Jie Jie went about showing Di Di their new shared bedroom. A room exploding with bluebird colored walls and pink and purple butterflies. A closet filled from floor to ceiling with poofy dresses, and pink clothes.

Di Di wandered from item to item stopping at the dresser.

On top of the dresser was a picture of Jie Jie in her hot pink sequined outfit, a Barbie in the traditional Chinese wedding *qi pao,* and a toy car. A toy car! In photos, you can almost see Di Di do a double take at that car.

And of everything in her new house, this is what Di Di chose to touch, and then clutch as she made her way with great hesitation to the closet. Jie Jie, excited to show off all the pretty things, was oblivious to Di Di's hesitation.

March 2008

Di Di spent the first few months in the United States copying Jie Jie in her dress and actions. Jie Jie loved all things pink and purple—the more glitz the better. For Di Di, this mimicking would soon end. As a three year old, Di Di learned English quickly and, like all kids, knew what she liked and desired. Soon enough, Di Di began to articulate very clearly in English, "I dress self mama!"

Indeed, from underwear to outfits, Di Di wanted to don only clothes with the traditional promotional characters traditionally reserved for boys. Although we searched and searched, little girls' panties do not come with images of Thomas the Tank Engine, Spiderman, or Diego the animal rescuer on them, so home we came with boys' underwear. Di Di was so proud of her new "panties" and proudly paraded around the house in nothing but.

Quickly all clothes were questioned. Swimsuits could only be trunks and swim shirts—with images of Nemo and Thomas, to be specific. Even T-shirts clearly had a gender in Di Di's mind. She was drawing a clear line in the sand.

The contents of Di Di's closet were quickly replaced to

match her independent, non-conforming style. In contrast to her sister's pink and purple, Di Di's new clothes were orange, blue and green. In preschool, Di Di only wanted to play with boys and participate in sports. This was another indication that Di Di did not conform to the gender norms for little girls expected in US society.

May 2008, Di Di's 4ᵗʰ Birthday

Di Di loves birthdays. Children do not have birthday parties in China, so this was Di Di's first. Di Di loved Diego and insisted on having a *Go Diego Go!* Scavenger Hunt Party.

The invitations clearly stated the following:

Gift ideas: Di Di loves all sports: soccer, baseball, basketball, tennis, golf, and hockey. Her favorite colors are orange, blue, and green. Some of her favorite animated characters include: Diego, Thomas, Spiderman, and Lightning McQueen. She loves books, puzzles, tools, Legos, and Tinker Toys.

The motivation for writing this came when Di Di received a gift from a relative. The gift, a dress, while fitting for most little girls, was not fitting for Di Di. She assumed it was not for her and handed it to Jie Jie. It broke my heart.

November 2008

Living in a cold weather state, the expectation to know how to skate and ski are steeped in tradition. Di Di had proved to be quite an athlete over the past year, excelling in soccer during the warmer months. Jie Jie and Di Di began ice-skating at the local training center.

The following June, the figure skating program ended with a professional ice performance including each child who had skated that year. Di Di's group, the four- and five-year-olds, would be skating with several professional skaters to Frank Sinatra's "New York, New York." In the lobby of the center was a picture of a famous skater from the 1950s wearing a top hat and tails. For this number the little girls' costumes mimicked those of French hotel maids, but the little boys' costumes were tuxedos. Di Di pointed to the man in the tuxedo and said she wanted to dress like that boy. With the conviction of a matador, I let the director know that Di Di had requested to wear the tuxedo costume. "The boy's costume?" the Director asked. I confirmed that my little girl wanted to wear the tuxedo. The Director looked at me and said that in sixteen years no parent has ever requested that their daughter wear the boys' costume. But…she needed more boys for the routine. Di Di was thrilled! She beamed in the tux and shone on the ice.

Two years later, and two sizes too small, the tuxedo costume is still worn in and out of the house regularly and proudly.

September 2009

Until this point Di Di had never gone to bed without me lying down with her. "Is there something I can do so you will go to sleep on your own?" I thought to ask her. "Yes," Di Di said, "if you make my room blue and red with soccer balls."

At the time, Jie Jie and Di Di shared a room and it was adorned with butterflies and was pink and purple from the curtains to the quilts, primarily because it had been decorated for our older daughter. I had never seen this as an issue before. But literally, as if I was living in a cartoon, a light bulb went off above my head.

The very next morning, I dropped Di Di off at preschool and went shopping. By the time Di Di returned home her half of the room was redecorated. Di Di's face lit up, and she could barely breathe. Stuttering, she exclaimed: "It is so beautiful Ma Ma. Thank you!" I cried, realizing that this is what is important: respecting the outside, the inside, and everything in between, even if it is not comprehensible to you at the moment.

January 2010

As Caucasian-Jewish parents, we had decided that along with learning Mandarin, we would incorporate all major Chinese holidays and customs into our children's lives. In the Chinese culture, *Xin Nian* (New Year's) or *Chuan Tian* (Spring Festival) is a time for renewal. There is a prescribed list of things you must do to prepare to purge the old and ensure a good, blessed, and prosperous year. For example, cleaning your home, buying new clothes, and cutting your hair are three important customs. All of our children look forward to the haircutting ritual.

This year at the salon, Di Di sat and thumbed through the "men's Japanese hair style book," and then pointed definitively to the poster of the male hair model on the wall whose hair was short and spiky. Di Di said, "I want that hair cut." Our experienced and kind stylist had owned a salon in Korea for over twenty years prior to coming to the US, and she had been cutting Di Di's hair since adoption. "This is boy hair cut," she said looking at me. Turning to Di Di, I asked again if this was what she wanted. "Yes, Ma Ma!" Di Di's hair was cut to her specification. Looking in the mirror, Di Di beamed! He could finally see himself fully for the first time.

This was one of my proudest *Ma Ma* moments, and the

first of many defining moments on our journey. As long as I live, I will never forget that look. At age five-and-a-half, Di Di was teaching me how someone can truly be themselves when they receive unconditional support.

March 2010

In March, when I was driving the kids to school, from the back seat Di Di firmly asked, "When am I going to grow my penis?"

As a child, I recall being called a tomboy; I climbed trees, played with boys, ran around in the woods behind my house, but I never once thought I was missing a part of my body. Never did I feel the need to assert that I was a boy or a girl. I was a girl that liked what I liked.

But this new question defined the difference. Di Di's question, clearly unprompted, articulated the incongruence of how he saw himself and how the world defined her.

In retrospect, I wish I had been wiser. I answered with a question. "If you could continue to dress like you want, and play with what you like, and do what makes you feel like you, even if you never grow a penis, would that make you happy?"

"Yes," Di Di replied.

"Phew," I thought. But I now understand that Di Di was asking: "Can I be a boy? Can I be the identity I feel I am—even if I do not have the matching parts now?"

July 2010

Eventually, we became a family of five. Jie Jie is eight, Ge Ge, our newly adopted son, is seven, and Di Di is six. Ge Ge and Di Di have been bonded since their adoption, brothers through and through.

November 2010

Today Di Di came home from school and asked me why we call him a *her* when he is a boy. This time, I was looking straight into her dark black inquisitive eyes and I asked, "Do you want to be called *he* and *him*?"

"Yes," replied Di Di.

"OK," I replied. "We will try, and if I make a mistake, you will tell me."

My husband was traveling in Asia that month. I called to let him know that the binary had caught up with us. The freedom to be nonconforming was over as our first grader learned the meaning behind the pronouns *he* and *she*. *He* and *she* clearly define the constraints of the English language, creating a binary that is used to justify discrimination toward the population of people who fit in neither constricting box.

December 2010

We met with Di Di's school principal. She began the meeting saying, "In my twenty years of teaching..." and ended with, "Di Di will grow out of it, if it is not encouraged." The school administrator and staff refused to acknowledge that any child could be born in a body that did not match their gender identity. I immediately knew I needed a new environment for my children.

I did not know what I know now. The state in which I live provides no laws of protection for my child to be who he is. Even scarier is the fact that in this state, simply allowing children to be who they are can be considered a criminal action. To know that the Civil Rights Act does not apply to my child is incomprehensible. I am horrified by the ignorance of those in charge of our public institutions. In contrast, I am struck by the complete wisdom Di Di, at age six, exudes. Di Di's conviction regarding his gender identity motivates me to act against every barrier placed in our way.

We were fortunate to meet another principal in our district, who offered us refuge without hesitation. She later told me that she had informed the district administrators that as a woman of color who had also experienced prejudice and discrimination in this school district, she refused to inflict the same on us or Di Di. Indeed, it was her business to educate children, and I had three children who would be educated and respected. Di Di was welcome to be introduced as a boy in first grade. And, he was. I am forever in her debt. She is my hero!

April 2011

Five months have passed, and Di Di is a fully gender-conforming boy. He continues to love life, he has many friends and succeeds in school. Because of the danger, Di Di remains "stealth," meaning we only discretionarily disclose. Di Di understands that some things—although not secret—are private.

In being allowed into the protective world of the transgender community, I have met and become close friends with men just like Di Di. There is no better way to feel acceptance than to find people like you. Di Di proudly refers to them all as the "boys with vaginas."

I will die trying to change unjust laws and to persuade the closed-minded to be more open. It shouldn't be this hard to support a child when they tell you who they are. Di Di's courage to remain true to who he is as a person is what keeps me moving forward.

Di Di is a happy child, a child with a love for life and an infectious laugh. Di Di exudes confidence beyond his chronological years, and I am truly blessed to be his *Ma Ma*.

Kate Levy's journey began in 1987 in a class called Women in Developing Countries. At eighteen, she knew she was connected to the larger world community, and that one day she would adopt a daughter from China. Today, twenty four years later, she has three incredible, beautiful, unique children from China.

Transition Mama

Kathleen Finn

He wrote an email: "I have never and do not feel like a girl/woman. I am going through a transition to be a man…"

I whirled mentally and emotionally. What does this mean for him? How will I tell people and what will they think? Feelings of confusion, insecurity, fear, and sadness, followed by a deep breath and the momentary clarity of a good first response: "I love you. Period. Everything else we can talk about over time." There was nothing more in my reply because, though a writer at heart, I did not know what else to write—then.

Now, two years have passed and I have learned a lot. For example, saying *he* instead of *she*—and quite naturally I have learned to call my baby by a new name after a motherhood-long use of another name. I have felt brokenhearted at not being able to discern his needs at a younger age, and for his pain at not being able to live as who he truly is earlier in his life. I have felt pride at his courage, for his humility in the face of overwhelming adversity. He has invited me into a remarkable journey of discovery: laying bare what it means to be fundamentally human, recognizing the roles our culture attempts to force on us, and exploring the possibilities beyond those roles.

He and I did not arrive here easily. Never an easy child, he was colicky as an infant, rebellious as a toddler, and hard to get out of bed for school almost every morning. Being who I am— my mother often told me, "You were such a happy baby!"—I found it tough to have a "difficult" child who always seemed unhappy. Adding to this, as a result of a divorce when he was three, we were financially distressed throughout his early childhood. An independent woman, I pursued a career while single-parenting a child I was struggling to understand.

A few fundamentals worked out well enough. His education was high quality, due to a bit of luck with public schools, the advantage of a private high school, the college scholarship awarded for his academic achievements, and the help of a good friend. Our relocation from the Midwest to the more liberal Northeast was propitious for his adolescent social life, as well as for my career development, which eased our financial circumstances over time.

However, his clinical depression diagnosis, accompanied by a suicide attempt, was a major heartbreak! By then I realized that I did not have an ordinary child. Though I did not try to define his sexuality, I can look back now and realize that I was not open to entertaining the question of his gender identity. Perhaps I could have interpreted signals differently. I wish I had

had access to educational or mental health resources on gender identity in adolescent development.

Despite these challenges, he found his own ways to explore these issues, and to this day I continue to be amazed at how he invited me into his evolving process. I witnessed and began to acknowledge his new self through his expressive interests in art and theater, even his choice of a major at college. Later, he began to bind his breasts, and introduce me to several female-to-male romantic partners. I knew something was up, but decided not to inquire about these developments, waiting for him to come to me with his understanding of himself as a female-to-male transgender person.

So, shortly after the email, we began to talk more openly about his transition, and our next challenges soon emerged. I was interested in his health, his safety, his nutritional needs, and what I could help with on a basic level. I just wanted to know that he was healthy, happy and whole, but he seemed to want me to ask him other kinds of questions. I still do not know what those are or were. He assisted with information on etiquette, language, and discourse; I read everything, eager to know what to do.

And I talked with people around me. I felt I was "coming out" as the parent of a transgender child. I am a public leader and I spoke face-to-face with trusted members of our community. I went around to visit workplace colleagues, many of whom had supported me in the past. Most were curious and supportive, though a few seemed taken aback. On one of my visits, I spoke with my siblings who lived in another state and learned that my nieces and nephews were generally more open than their parents of my generation. In all of these conversations, I tried to respond honestly to their questions while drawing appropriate boundaries. I expressed my pride in my child's courage to be who he truly is, affirming that as the principle we all want for our children.

One of the more difficult exchanges took place with my domestic partner who was uneasy about accepting my son's transgender friends and partners into our home. My son and he had never been interested in a parent–child relationship, and I had accepted that over the years since we are great companions to each other. However, their relational distance proved challenging for me.

In response, I first tried something that did not work well. I staged an evening of conversation with a good friend, a local minister who is himself a transgender person. My partner, my son, a good male friend of my partner's, and I all gathered in the living room. I hoped someone would find a way into a difficult conversation, and my partner would realize how congenial this all could be. Nothing substantive came of it, though we had a nice enough casual visit.

So I had to be very direct in talking with my partner. When I told him about my son's transition and my whole-hearted support for his transition, I stated my boundaries very clearly: "You are free, of course, to think whatever you like. But when you speak to me and others in our home, I will not tolerate ridicule or negative language about transgender people in general, or about my son in particular. If you cannot abide by this, it will be a dealbreaker for me. It means we cannot go on together, because this is my child's well being and I cannot compromise on this."

I felt quite vulnerable, but very clear about my position.

Slowly, surely, without further discussion, he began to refer to my son by his new name, to use masculine pronouns, and to correct himself when he used the incorrect pronoun or name. He has never again uttered a pejorative phrase about any transgender person in my presence.

All this was in advance of what I like to call our "transition odyssey," the cross-country trip we took so my son could have chest reconstruction surgery. By the time we were discussing surgery, I knew I had to help. I was pained by his wearing chest binding every day, and haunted by what that must be doing to his body, especially since testosterone supplements were changing his bones. My son's partner, himself a veteran of this surgery, rounded out our crew of transition voyagers.

I bankrolled the transportation, food and lodging, while my son's partner did the hands-on medical care and support. It was a perfect configuration. With a false start on the lodging arrangements, we spent the night before surgery in a strange city driving around looking for a new place to stay for the next five days. The surgery was a great success and we had a memorable trip.

As I reach the end of this essay, I feel a bit like I have failed to convey the struggle and adversity of being a "transition parent." Instead I am amazed at how love has energized our family relationships, activating our human capacity for change and adaptation. I have probed the mystery of transition and its personal, cultural, and global consequences. My son and I exchange "I love you" more easily. My partner and I embrace change with greater resilience. In response to a harsh world around us, we have worked harder to support one another. And life itself—this magnificent adventure with transitions wrought by adversity, aging, economics, weather, and unexpected surprises—is a more engaging medley of transitions for my son, my partner, my siblings, my friends, and me, all navigating through it together.

Kathleen Finn works in education, community organizing and nonprofit management. She serves as an elected official for her home community. Her passion for environmental activism steers her choice of paid work and volunteer activities toward those focused on open space, human health, nutritional resilience, sustainable transportation, faith-based ecology, and respect for all life and life-support systems.

Our Story

Sharon Brown

I didn't know I was expecting a little boy, but after being fourteen days late, I had a normal labor, and there he was. At eight pounds, two ounces, Nick was perfect in every way.

Nick was a happy little boy. Affectionate and outgoing, he hit all the normal markers, and was on his feet by thirteen months. He used his newfound mobility to make his own choices. Despite all attempts to interest him in footballs, trucks and cars, by the time Nick was eighteen months old, he was wearing jumpers on his head to simulate long hair and was dressing up in my shoes and skirts. At that stage it was cute, but by the time he was two, he refused to play with boys' toys, and a little niggle was telling me that this wasn't the sort of behavior I was seeing in other little boys. But I didn't worry too much. I was sure it was just a phase.

By the time Nick started nursery school at two-and-a-half, I had realized that he wasn't a typical boy. But who cared? So he liked Barbie and My Little Pony. One day the nursery staff pulled me to the side and told me that Nick only played with the girls, and at dressing up time, he was fighting to get to the special little black dress. I told them it was fine, and to let him get on with it. I knew already what he preferred.

His father, Tim, was having a harder time, struggling with this little boy who wasn't interested in football or rough play. At one point Tim confiscated all of Nick's toys and told him he had to play with boy things. All that did was make our son miserable, so after a few months Tim relented.

By the time Nick was four years old, I realized that this "phase" was lasting a very long time. I spoke to our family doctor, but he didn't have a clue about what to do. He suggested that we wait and see, as Nick was very young and would probably grow out of this phase. Hmm. That didn't work out too well.

At around age four-and-a-half, just after starting primary school, Nick told me that God had made a mistake, and that he should have been made a girl. Although I knew he liked girl things and had told him this was perfectly OK, this statement hit me like a ton of bricks. My son was starting to understand that other children didn't feel the same way he did, and it was making him miserable.

At six years old, on the way to school one morning, Nick asked me when he could have the operation to chop off his willy and give him a fanny. I nearly crashed the car! But when I explained that an operation like that would only happen after he was grown up, he was devastated. He wanted it now.

I looked for information online, and found Mermaids, an organization for the families of transgender children in England. I realized that I wasn't alone with this; my son wasn't the only little boy who felt this way. The organization put me in touch with other parents who could relate to how I was feeling. I also asked our family doctor for a referral for Tavistock, a special clinic in London.

At the same time, because I could see my child becoming more and more unhappy, I began to buy non-boys' clothes for him to wear at home. Not dresses, but sparkly jeans and colorful girls' tops. Telling him that he was a boy who liked girls' things wasn't helping; he simply replied that he was a girl inside, and I finally decided to listen to him. He was so happy it made me cry, but I felt as if everyone in the shop was watching and judging me for buying girls' clothes for my little boy.

At Tavistock, we were told that this wasn't my fault, and the clinician diagnosed Nick with Gender Identity Disorder. The therapists finally made Tim realise that this was not anyone's doing, and we discussed that there was a reasonable possibility that Nick would not change his mind about his identity. This was a turning point for me, as I realized that if I didn't stick up for Nick and try to let him be who he wanted to be, who would? Eventually Tim and I split up, which had nothing to do with Nick. But, this meant I had more freedom to let Nick be himself at home. I bought him more girls' clothes, shoes, handbags, and, eventually, dresses. When we were at home, he could wear what he wanted, and if he wanted the butterfly face paint, then he got it. He could wear dresses inside the house, and to family parties. My family listened to what I said, and they respected Nick's right to be whom he wanted.

Unfortunately, things were different at school. He was still wearing boy clothes at school, and was becoming increasingly depressed and isolated. He told the other children he had a girl brain in a boy body, which is, in my opinion, true. Unfortunately, Nick's attendance was suffering as he was staying home due to being bullied. The school tried to deal with it, but Nick ran away from school on a number of occasions, because he was so unhappy. The only place he could be himself was at home.

By the time Nick was nine, I realized that despite advice to the contrary, I couldn't keep forcing him to live as someone he wasn't. He had already told all the other children that he was really a girl, and I made the decision to let him dress in whatever he wanted, and to grow his hair. We changed pronouns shortly thereafter. The school was not happy, but again the Tavistock team came down and helped them to address the issues, such as safe toilet use, P.E., and the bullying. In her last year at primary school, now living as Nicky, my daughter was the happiest she had been since starting school.

Allowing Nicky to live as a girl made a huge difference to her behavior at home and at school. Her attendance went back to normal, she was happy and productive in class, and she was a much nicer person to be around. The hoped-for change of mind did not seem to be materializing, and I started to prepare myself for the fact that Nicky might stay Nicky. I found out that medication called hormone blockers could be given to put puberty on hold. I also found out that this treatment was not permitted at Tavistock until age sixteen. I was horrified. It didn't make sense to me that Nicky would be forced to go through a male puberty just to prove that it wasn't what she wanted.

I contacted a well-known Dutch team to ask if they would

treat her in their program, but they said that although she fit all the criteria, she wasn't a Dutch national so they couldn't include her. I looked into buying the blockers online, and was then introduced to Dr. Norman Spack from the Boston Children's Hospital in the US, who agreed to treat Nicky. This treatment could start when she reached the right stage of puberty, which would be the developmental stage known as Tanner Stage 2.

At this time, Nicky also started secondary school, and it was a disaster. She was spat at, punched, kicked, and on multiple occasions had groups of older children surrounding her shouting insults. Within three months of starting secondary school, she took an overdose of drugs. After the second over-dose attempt, I began to home-school her. However, she was bored at home, and we tried again to integrate her back into school. More attempted overdoses followed. Nicky was finding early puberty incredibly distressing. She self-harmed, and hated her changing body. After fighting for months to get Nicky seen either by the Dutch or at Tavistock, I booked flights to Boston to go see Dr. Spack.

Tim, Nicky, and I went to see Dr. Spack just after Nicky turned thirteen. She was well into the developmental stage of puberty known as Tanner 2, nearly Tanner 3, but thank-fully we got there before she experienced any major changes, such as facial hair or voice change. To say meeting Norman was wonderful really doesn't do the whole experience justice. He was simply amazing. He was incredibly gracious to Nicky, and told her that under no circumstances would he let her go through a male puberty. He prescribed blockers and he told her that he wanted to see her again in six months, and he told me of a number of tests that he would need us to organize, and then send him the results. Nicky had told me she would rather be dead than become more male, and I believed her. She would not be here today if I had not taken her to Norman.

We went to Boston every six months to see Norman, and he prescribed estrogen when Nicky was nearly fourteen to stop her growth. He estimated that even with blockers she would be over six feet if she didn't have estrogen to fuse her bone plates. Without estrogen and blockers, her estimated final height would have been around six foot four inches. She is just under six feet now.

School improved when the local Education Welfare officer found Nicky a place at a small unit that dealt with children with long term illness, or, as in Nicky's case, had been traumatized because of bullying. Once she started here, as a girl, with nobody any the wiser about her history, she became much happier and more settled.

Those years now seem like a long distant nightmare. Life is normal, Nicky is happy, and is getting on with her life. She has a boyfriend who knows her history, and she is currently working two part time jobs while looking for full time work. I have a happy, outgoing teenage girl, who steals my perfume and my makeup—not my clothes, I am not trendy enough for her—and has a full social life and a doting boyfriend. Wherever she goes, people look at her because she is beautiful, not because she was obviously born male. She doesn't have a deep voice, Adams apple, a male facial structure or excess body or facial hair. She is a reasonable height for a woman—she loves being nearly six feet tall—and if you met her today, you would be shocked to discover that she was born with male genitalia.

Nicky has had sex reassignment surgery (SRS), so she

doesn't need to go see Norman anymore, but I consider him to be her savior, and ours, as well. I can't imagine how life would have been if Norman had not been there for us, and I am glad I don't have to. I am certain it would be a life without my daughter in it.

Sharon Brown is a single Mum to four wonderful kids, working in IT in the North of England. She has a large and loving family, and a great job. She feels her life is good, and she enjoys spending time with friends and family, reading, watching films, and drinking red wine.

From A M to P M

Georgia Myers

My upbringing was very hard. At the tender age of seventeen, my mother, Ethel, gave birth to me and left me with her mother, Hattie, who was a prostitute. I never had a stable home life, and I was constantly bounced around from family to family, and very badly abused.

Luckily, I tuned out to be a good person, thank God, and well liked by everyone who knows me. I got married in 1962, was married for nineteen years, and had three beautiful children. Looking back, I feel that I was the best wife and mother that I could be, and I took care of my children well. My husband and I divorced in 1991. My children and I have a great relationship and to this day they show a lot of love toward their mother.

When my transgender child Amber, now Preston, was growing up, I knew she was different from other children. As young as ages four or five, Amber always liked to play with boys' toys and never liked dresses. And she always wanted to wear warm–up pants.

Years later, Amber came to my work one day and visited with me over lunch. She said that she had something to discuss with me. Then she asked me if I noticed that she was often staying with friends rather than staying at home. The reason, she explained, was that she was seeing another woman. "I am gay," she told me.

At first I was taken aback by this news. I asked her when she discovered that she was gay. She said that she had always felt different, and that eventually she knew she wanted to be with a woman. I asked her, "Don't you like men, also?" She replied, "Yes, somewhat." But she added that she was mostly trying to figure out who she was.

Well I have always accepted my child no matter what he wanted to do in life. As long as life for him is good, and he's not being hassled or harassed by anyone, I have no problem with him being gay or transgender. I love Preston and always will because he is my flesh and blood. My love for him will never change. If anything it's gotten stronger. Preston's friends feel no different.

However, I do have concerns about Preston having his breasts removed. I do know that his being transgender is not a choice, and further understand that for some transgender people it is mandatory to have their bodies match what their hearts feel. I have told him that he'd better make sure that this is really what he wants, because if he has that surgery, there will be no turning back. I have also heard that sometimes very bad scar tissue can result from this type of operation. But if this is what he still wants to do, I will support him one-hundred percent.

I continue to have a hard time calling him by his chosen name, Preston. The name he was given at birth, Amber, still rings in my head. It's not that I don't want to call him Preston; I am OK with that name. But as a parent, the name you chose for your child at birth just sort of stays with you, and rolls off your tongue when you least expect it.

At first, this transformation was very hard for Preston's older son. He used to stress about what his friends would think, or what they would say about him when they found out the person he was calling his mother now looked like a person he should be calling his father. When he finally came to the conclusion that the people around him were fine with it, he was better able to accept it. Preston's younger son had an easier time dealing with it. Both of them dearly love Preston, whom they know as their mother, and will likely always call him *Mom*. This is because he is still their mother, and I believe that Preston wouldn't have it any other way. But Preston now has a beautiful granddaughter whom he is crazy about, and she will be raised knowing him as "Boppy"—her grandfather.

I think parents should stand by their children no matter what life they choose to live. I do feel sorry for those families who do not accept, and even disown their gay or transgender children. They are their own flesh and blood! Their children are human beings and have feelings. Don't throw them to the wolves. Lastly, I would tell other parents to love their children unconditionally, no matter what.

From AM to PM

Georgia Myers is an African-American woman who grew up Baptist in a small town called Littleton, North Carolina.

Living Between Two Worlds

Anonymous

When you have children, you want the best for them. You want them to grow up healthy, happy and well-adjusted. You want the American Dream for them: a house, a car, and a family that loves them.

But what happens when your child tells you they're altering their body and their life and becoming someone of the opposite sex? What you should do is adjust and change with them. Looking back over the past ten years, I realize I didn't do that. I feel like I failed my child for my lack of acceptance and support, and failed myself by being rigid and inflexible in my personal beliefs.

My transgender child went from female to male around thirty-two years of age. This was extremely difficult for me to accept. I'd been raised hard-shell Southern Baptist, so it was quite a struggle! I actually went through a period of mourning because I felt my daughter had died when she became a man. I just resisted this change in every conceivable way. I even became upset with the hospital where he received his counseling and sex-change surgery. When I get up enough nerve, one day I intend to apologize for my resistance to my child's transition and for how this affected him. Hopefully, he'll be understanding and tolerant with me as I struggle through this. He has been so far.

My child didn't feel comfortable talking to me about his decision to transition. I'm betting this is not uncommon. For a long time, I felt as if my child had died. To top it all off, I was quite rude when he brought a special friend to visit. This was the person who would later become his life partner, only I didn't know it at the time. Rudeness is unforgivable for a person brought up in the South during the sixties, as I was!

But my husband and older son kept reminding me that this is still my child, so I should not shut him out. After not speaking for a long time, I began to miss talking to my youngest one. The baby I gave birth to was now a young adult and able to make his own life decisions. Not being needed was lonely. So after what I remember as a very long time, I did reach out to talk, and our conversation about this finally began. He told me he was still the same person and had not died, as I had felt. He was still "there," even though he had transitioned. He had just changed a little. He no longer had to pretend to be someone he didn't want to be. And my child was happier! This really shattered all of my preconceived ideas and challenged the upbringing I'd had.

For many years, I didn't tell anyone about my child's transition. At first I was in denial myself and never acknowledged their life change. When I did begin to acknowledge it, I was too busy dealing with accepting it myself to consider how others would take it. Eventually though, people were told.

For the most part, my friends are just glad that my child has someone to love him and is content and happy in his new life. But some of the people I told were actually horrified and couldn't get away from me fast enough. One woman in particular sticks in my mind. She is French Canadian and in the church every time its door opens. She is also the most critical person in the church and the most unforgiving, which is why I never wanted to tell her. Her reaction when it finally did come to light was expected: she told me my child was going to hell. She refused to call my child by his new chosen name. She told me, "I've known God for most of my life and I understand what the Bible says will happen to those who are gay."

Yes, I was going to cut off all ties with this woman unless her attitude changed. We'd known each other for over two decades. I thought Christianity was about acceptance and forgiveness. But what had my child done that needed forgiveness? Nothing. Transitioning from one sex to another is condemned by many in the world, and men and women they've never met want to kill transgender people for it. That hurts deeply. I can't change the world but I can change my attitude.

We play back the tapes in adulthood we learned as children. But we can also change the content of those tapes. It takes a lot of will power and practice to change the way you think. It's like a stoplight. Every time you catch yourself in the old habits, just visualize a stoplight and STOP! Then re-think the way you're going. It's as simple and as hard as that.

After that conversation, I underwent more intense soul-searching to clarify what I wanted for my kids. I want my children to be happy and find someone to love them, whether or not I understand it. Would it be the American Dream or their happiness? Their happiness won out.

In the end, I realized that this was my child and I needed to accept him for who he wanted to be. He is happy and content being himself, rather than who or what I wanted him to be. Love won out after a difficult struggle. After all, straight people don't exactly have a monopoly on getting love right either. I'm just grateful that he has someone to love him.

Yes, my child found someone special to share his life with, and they have now presented us with a grandchild. He's absolutely adorable and any conflict between the adults has just dissolved with this little new addition to our family. It's all about acceptance and love, something the world just doesn't have enough of.

In conclusion and as advice to anyone struggling with this issue as I did, I'd like to say that your child may simply be a lovely spirit trapped in the wrong body. Please don't ask them to be less than they are. Continue to love and support them and change with them. You don't have to change your philosophy about their transition, just be tolerant of it and don't condemn them for it. If you think it's hard for you, have you thought about how hard it is for them? Life is hard enough without making it harder for others. I feel very strongly that we must leave this world a better place than it was before us. Think about it. If you already are, then you've started the journey of acceptance.

Transitions of the Heart

The author was raised "hard-shell" Southern Baptist, so it was extremely challenging for her to accept her child's transition. Because of privacy concerns, she has chosen to remain anonymous.

He Is Finally Living His Dream

Betti Shook

I didn't have many preconceived ideas about how to parent my kids, but I did want to be the kind of mother to my daughter that I always wished I had. Unlike my own mother, who suffered from schizophrenia while I was growing up, I wanted to be fully present.

Though my mother's mental illness was no fault of her own, as a child I longed for a female counterpart to teach me how to be in the world. So as an adult, I was determined to be the mother who would take her daughter to ballet, do her hair, teach her how to sew, cook, and be a mom. I especially wanted my two kids to feel safe and to know that they always had a safe haven at home with me.

Despite her illness, my own mother was able to teach me

the most important part of life, and that was to love deeply and completely. To be certain that those around you are aware that you love them and are there to support them no matter what. Though loving, I was stern and demanding with my children. I think being Catholic influenced my childrearing approach more than I realized. Yet this also instilled a sense of community in my kids, and I think this helped form who they are today. Both my children say they felt loved, and that they learned the difference between right and wrong, and to respect their fellow human beings.

My greatest fear and regret is that this longing may have put too much pressure on my oldest child, Alic, who was born female but transitioned to male. I now realize that all children are born exactly as they are meant to be. As parents, all we need to do is help them become the people they were intended to be. Maybe this love is what got us through the transition.

Certainly Alic's transition hasn't been easy for any of us, and his father and brother are still coming to terms with it. In fact, Alic's father and I divorced during this time. Alic's transition has made me question a number of things I thought I knew. But what I *do* know is that my child, who since the age of three seemed to be so uncomfortable with his place in the world, is finally content and peaceful.

Alic spent his early years being shy, and I think I may have pushed him too hard to get him over this phase. Then he became overly boisterous and loud, which made it hard on all of us. Alic went to a Catholic elementary school, a Fundamentalist Christian high school, and then ended up at Mills College where he was finally able to begin addressing so many of his conflicted feelings. He transitioned right out of college.

I first noticed something might be different about Alic when he was around age three or four. He saw me sewing and literally cried out, "No more pinafores, Mom, please!" Another moment of recognition came when Alic was in junior high. All the other girls were trying to catch the attention of the boys, but Alic was trying to beat them on the soccer field! There were actually a lot of moments like this, if I think about it. A leader known for being tenacious, Alic was an extremely competitive player, which seemed to fit a pattern. Often, everyone in the family gave into Alic just because it was the easiest thing to do given his strong will. And even though Alic couldn't walk through the mall without heads turning—she was an absolutely gorgeous young woman—it was very hard for Alic to feel like she was a part of the female world.

Alic had many years of anxiety and we were all concerned. I was worried that he might become so despondent he would attempt suicide. How was it for me? Years of tears. Nothing I'll ever let Alic know. I was incredibly worried about him. In fact, when he was studying in Thailand on a Fulbright Scholarship, I traveled there just to confirm for myself that he was okay. And that is where he told me what he had decided to do.

I look back on that moment in a park in Thailand, watching the Komodo dragons and thinking that this wasn't how my life was supposed to transpire. I do remember some discomfort, as I still thought this was about me! I suppose it was strange, and somewhat selfish, for me to actually think this was about me and not him. Yet, it was a relief for both of us to finally share his plan. He just needed to know that he would be loved, and I needed to know that my child was and would be fine.

Alic wasn't one to give up on succeeding in anything he

attempted, and I believe that others in the same place need to know that their inner strength will give them courage, if they choose to draw on it. Still, it was an incredible struggle for both of us to get through this.

Mostly, however, I am so glad that he has finally found peace, and is capable of feeling satisfied with who he is. I'm so proud that through all the torment he went through, he has overcome so much, and now is living his dream.

Betti Shook grew up Catholic, the only child of a paranoid schizophrenic mother and a philandering father. She feels it is amazing that she grew up to be halfway normal. She is a Brands Development Director in the food brokering business, and has two children, Mike and Alic.

I'm Not Isabelle, I'm Isaboy

Tracie Stratton

My child is now ten. He transitioned at the age of five. By eighteen months I knew that this child, my fourth daughter, was different from the first three. In particular, she was very boyish, a characteristic which I had never thought about much before. Until Izzy, there were a lot of things I never thought about.

One of Izzy's first sentences, even before she was two, was, "Me a boy, Mama." I thought her confusion was cute. By the age of three, I discussed the issue with our pediatrician. By age five, I was in the doctor's office again, and consulting a psychiatrist. The psychiatrist, who came with great credentials and was the head of the pediatric psych association here in Oregon, had no clue how to handle the situation. Our final meeting with him concluded with him stating: "For God's sake, just let her be a lesbian." Of course by this time I knew that gender and sexual identity were two different things. I was upset that there was so little help for children like mine, nor did I know of any other children like mine.

I then went to an endocrinologist, who drew some blood from Izzy for lab work. When discussing the results, we found that my child had been making both sets of hormones, estrogen and testosterone, in equal parts. We learned that in a child so young, however, hormones can ebb and flow, and that this was not conclusive to anything. So what could we think? The endocrinologist said our child was transgender, but that we should not let a lab test alter our path. In short, we should continue to do what is right for Izzy.

So what was right for Izzy? I had no idea. I consulted the Internet and found a gender therapist, who in turn recommended a child specialist. This specialist, Cat Pivetti, has been and continues to be our lifesaver, helping us navigate life with an intersexed, transgender child. As a result, Izzy feels loved and confident about who he is.

My parents and siblings were great through the whole thing. My current husband, Izzy's step dad, was on board before me, and his parents have been supportive as well. The only person who had great difficulty with the transition was my ex-husband. In part due to our differences around supporting Izzy's gender expression, a terrible custody battle ensued. I am happy to say that I gained full custody. My ex spent several years in therapy himself, and, after almost six years, was able to accept Izzy completely. Their relationship has grown as a result. I realize that it is not very often when a custody battle involving a transgender child goes as well as mine did. Luckily, I utilized a great lawyer, a therapist, and a parent coordinator, all who worked very hard. It definitely paid off for Izzy, and for our entire family.

In some ways, and to many observers, my child's transition seemed to have happened overnight. But Izzy has always been a boy dressed like a girl. Kindergarten was the beginning of the transition, and it really hit home when we realized he was having difficulty navigating bathrooms there. In fact, he would rather have peed his pants than use the girls' restroom. At one point we were told Izzy wanted to be a boy because he saw this as strength and power. I knew in my heart Izzy did not want to be a boy, he *was* a boy—a boy trapped in a girl's body.

By Christmas time of that first school year, my child was extremely depressed. He never played with other kids at school, because he didn't fit in with the girls or the boys. In fact, most kids had a hard time telling what Izzy was: a boy dressed like a girl or a very boyish girl.

Around this time, Izzy would lay in bed every night and tell me he was a boy. He'd say, "God made a mistake," or ask, "Why does God hate me?" He also asked questions like "Why won't my penis pop out, it hurts up there" and even, "Am I going to be an abominable snow man?" (This last question stemmed from Izzy unfortunately overhearing a conversation in which one of the church ladies stated that Izzy was "an abomination of God.") I had no idea how to answer all of his questions.

I knew the therapy we had originally tried was failing, because my child was more and more unhappy, and, in retrospect, possibly suicidal. And then one Sunday it happened. We are not churchgoers, but my ex-husband attends a church that is not exactly "welcoming." The kids were with my ex, who was trying to put a dress on Izzy to get ready for church. After tantrums from both my ex-husband and Izzy, Tyfany, Izzy's older sister, found Izzy standing in the middle of a somewhat busy street. When she asked him what he was doing, he said he would rather die than be a girl. I realized then that I had a suicidal five-year-old child who needed help.

So, I started letting Izzy be a boy at home, wearing whatever clothes he wanted, and playing with whatever toys he chose. Most of these things had previously been removed from our home after some really bad advice from ill-informed "experts." We had been trying for a while to have everything be "female" around the house, and we even created a special "girls' club." I think Izzy would have loved to have been a girl just so this terrible nightmare would end. In fact, he really tried to act like a girl for a while to appease us, yet would always say things like, "See I could make a cute girl if I wanted to, but I'm really a boy." It took a while for us to really get that message.

One day my husband, Izzy's stepdad Buzz, was having a hard time getting Izzy ready for school. He decided to just let Izzy wear the boys' shirt with the car on it that day. His message on my phone went something like, "Honey don't be mad, I know we said not to let Izzy wear boys' clothes out of the house, but I had to get the kid to school." Later there was another message: "You're not going to believe this, but Izzy is playing with other kids! It's amazing. I can't believe it." Izzy never played with other kids; he never had friends. Not a girl and not a "real" boy, Izzy never fit in and usually felt isolated and depressed. It seemed as though this were about to change.

When I asked Izzy later if he was teased that day for wearing boys' clothes, he replied that only one kid had said anything, and it was only to tell him he was wearing a boys' shirt. No teasing ever ensued.

By that spring Izzy had transitioned, and later that summer, we used only male pronouns when referring to him. Izzy was so happy, and we had a huge birthday party of all his friends from school. This was the turning point. Many of the kids' parents who attended did not have a clue about Izzy's gender, and some people were upset by this. Was Izzy a boy or a girl? I have had many conversations like this along the way.

I knew I would have a rough road ahead, particularly when it came to school and my ex-husband. And I did have moments of really missing my daughter Isabelle, who in reality was never there. I always had the same child. Where was my mind? How could I miss a little girl who was never a little girl?

Now, my kids and I are so close. The whole experience has bonded us as a family. I learned so much about myself and how strong "just a mom" can be. When facing folks like school directors, I go in with my head held high and tell them what my child needs, instead of them telling me. I have consulted with transgender experts and have worked hard at Izzy's school educating administrators and parents about what transgender means, about my child's legal rights and what is and is not OK to ask or say.

This hasn't been easy, but I have stayed strong, kept my guard up, and continued to intervene before any problem ever touches my child. My child is unaware of the many meetings it takes to keep his life safe.

It has been almost six years since my child began his transition at school. He continues to use the boys' restroom, he plays on an all-boys' basketball team, and he is completely recognized as a boy. There has never been teasing, nor bullying.

We live in a small town, and at one point, everyone was aware of my child being "different." I know this is very challenging for many parents of trans children. But if you are a nice person, and let people know that this sort of thing happens, and that you are doing what the experts say is in the best interest of your child, they tend to shut up. I don't ask people what's between their child's legs, and they don't ask me about Izzy.

This last fall, Izzy had an implant placed, which will last for a year, to stop puberty. We plan on letting Izzy call the shots when it comes to hormones and all that. Izzy checks in with his very supportive therapist once a month and I believe it's still very important for Izzy to talk regularly to a professional whom he has known for years.

I also want Izzy to know he is not alone, so he has frequent play dates with other children like him, and we always go to gender conferences. I also use two web groups to help me through the experience.

I think parents of trans kids are the best parents ever. They unconditionally love their children, even when they don't completely understand what their child is going through. So, my advice to other parents is really just to love their child, no matter what, and to stay strong. This is not about you or your religion and beliefs; it's about your child. And get a great therapist, and an even better lawyer. Never let anyone question you. If your child is happy and a nice person, then you are doing the right thing.

Tracie Stratton was raised in Oregon with religious beliefs that are nondenominational, but include a touch of Catholic and New Age spirituality. Her childhood was good. She has very tolerant parents, who never spanked her, and tried to be as nonjudgmental as they could be. This helped her to accept all her children and love them in an unconditional way.

We Have All Come to Peace With It

Sue

Yet another operation for my child. For me, a sense of exasperation, combined with a lot of worry. My transgender daughter says she's still not right, still doesn't look a hundred percent like a woman. She has gone through gender reassignment surgery, cosmetic shaving of the jaw line and nose, and two hair transplants. She now says that the bones of her eyebrows and the hairline are not right.

This is the last operation, she assures me. "I have to be completely happy with myself," she says. I wonder if it will actually be the last. Or will it just be another £5000 down the drain? Or maybe now she will actually be content, and move on with her life. Apart from the gender reassignment surgery, the costs of which were covered by the National Health Service

(NHS), she's had to pay for it all herself. Consequently she has been living extremely frugally, which has made us worry that she has been depriving herself in other areas at the expense of her transition.

She still stares endlessly in the mirror, still sees things no one else sees, and I grieve for her. To her family, she looks fantastic—an attractive young thirty-two-year-old female. Her hair is somewhat thin, but how many women are perfect? How many of us are a hundred percent ultra femme? Will she ever be satisfied? Will she ever be happy? Will there always be some flaw that she sees, but no one else notices?

My child grew up here in England in what I consider to be a liberal, open-minded family. Her father and I were young adults during the hippie period, with no religious persuasion. Anything and everything was acceptable, and we believed in few boundaries. For our three children, this included the wearing of their sibling's clothes, and crossover behavior was indulged.

Maybe this is why we were not initially aware of gender problems for our daughter. In a more traditional family, perhaps this issue would have manifested sooner. This period also saw the rise of women's liberation. For a time my husband blamed our child's problems on feminism, which he saw as undermining men's role in the family and society.

At school, there were the usual pressures to conform, and our child behaved as a normal boy in all outward appearances. He had, however, a slightly odd shape, rather plump, with small breasts and somewhat feminine nipples. How he hated school swimming sessions! He was also somewhat reticent and shy, always running away from problems.

At the age of fifteen, our child announced that *she* was in the wrong body. We knew so little about the condition we couldn't believe she could be transgender. We were just a normal, regular family. My husband had difficulty believing that this condition actually existed. He saw her as simply a boy who was scared of the stereotypical male role, combined with the normal identity problems of adolescence.

At seventeen, she tried to overdose on drugs. After the overdose, our child saw a psychiatrist on two occasions. He was not very sympathetic, saying she simply had obsessive compulsive tendencies. The psychiatrist said nothing at all about her being transgender.

I spent endless walks with our transgender daughter talking it through. At first, my husband and I tried to deny the reality of her possibly being transgender. We both tried so hard to persuade her, and ourselves, that it wasn't real. We paid for her to see a different psychiatrist, all to no avail. It was all so difficult. I went to my doctor for advice. I was told there was none forthcoming. As my child was over the age of consent, it was up to her and her doctor to determine what to do. There was no help offered for us, the parents, in terms of understanding or counseling.

Eventually my child went to university to study cartography, a subject she had been fascinated with since childhood. Within a month she was home again saying she couldn't bear to be in a program that was predominately male. She then attended a college of further education, and after another year of study, she reapplied to another university to study sociology. Here the majority of students were women, but she still felt she didn't fit in. She was still operating as a man at this point. She was so full of hate and anger towards women. I wondered if it was jealousy.

It was then, much to our relief, that our child met a foreign university student. She was a lovely girl who was very understanding. She had some of her own problems, but our son/daughter was always there for her. "He" was so considerate of her. We all hoped our child's problems would now go away. When our child was twenty-six, her partner became pregnant. They were so proud and happy. Our daughter had always wanted to have children. We were happy too, and our relief was enormous. We naively believed her problems would now recede.

However, panic and paranoia set in with our daughter. Her hair was thinning, and she felt that she couldn't be a woman with thinning hair. How could her children grow up thinking she wasn't a woman?

Naively, we had thought that the birth of twin daughters would sort her out, that is, give her a positive role as a father. However, two months after their birth she was taking hormones she had purchased from the Internet. In no way were her children to grow up thinking she was a man. She was totally obsessed. It was incredibly hard for her partner, and for us. We were full of mixed emotions: anger, distress, and pain. How could she do this now, with a partner still recovering from childbirth, and with twins? Her father more or less rejected her. It was a bad time. She also hated us for what she perceived as our lack of support. However, her partner continued to be supportive, an amazing woman indeed.

Now, five years on, after much pain, grief, and alienation, not only from us, her parents, but also from her siblings, we have all finally accepted the reality of the situation. We have come to peace with it, if you like. The question of whether she was born this way, or whether something in her childhood triggered it, has become irrelevant.

The gender reassignment surgery was in some ways a relief. After that, there was no turning back. We all had to move on; there seemed no point in discussing it any further. At the time, the operation and convalescence was horrendous, and we had worries she might have regrets. However, it became obvious that her only feelings were of relief. It was now all sorted, over and done with. And to the relief of our trans-daughter, her father, who had fought against her situation all along, now finally accepted it and became a rock of strength. Our relationship with our daughter is so much better now, and so much of the grief, pain, anger, and anguish of the past has now turned into awe, respect, and pride.

True, my husband and I still have problems with pronouns, and often lapse when talking to each other, but we pull each other up over it. It's still difficult to tell people. Close friends know, and we are lucky in that all have been supportive.

However, I still ask myself if our daughter will ever feel satisfied with her appearance. Today she is much more relaxed about things, much more comfortable in her female persona. We know that only a remarkable, amazing person with such determination could transition so successfully.

Yet the odd stare is still treated as suspect, and I do wonder if that will ever go away. Will there be more operations? After her recent surgery, she looks amazing to us—one-hundred percent female.

The differences between male and female seem to be so

immense, yet so small. Just small tweaks here and there and everything is different. We also wonder if the lack of testosterone in her body has taken away any drives and passions she might have had, as she has become remarkably flat in personality. We find this apparent lack of emotion difficult to accept. She is highly intelligent, but the self-obsession, paranoia, and the avoidance of society which seems to go with her condition, has taken its toll. We are all hoping that she will now finally move on with her life.

Sue lives in a large town in the East Midlands of the UK. She is in her sixties, in good health, and married. Her transgender daughter is the youngest of her children; she has two other children, an older son and daughter. She has five grandchildren, two of whom are the children of her transgender daughter. She works part-time as an artist and lecturer.

My Daughter Was Always Different

Ann Ferraiolo

I knew my daughter was different from a very young age. As a toddler she would never play with dolls, but gravitated towards toys like trucks and cars. She would cry uncontrollably when I would try to get her to wear feminine clothing. She wouldn't wear dresses, or let me put bows in her hair, and she only ever wanted to wear pants.

At the age of twelve, she got her first period. I remember that day like it was yesterday. I heard this horrifying scream coming from the bathroom. She was hysterically shrieking, "No, I don't want this!" I was so confused, as I thought that girls were usually happy when they got their first period. But our daughter was always different.

Things just got worse from there. My husband and I

noticed that she was becoming angrier, and she began to isolate herself from everyone. Her school grades dropped from A's and B's to D's and F's. This was mainly because she refused to go to school. We didn't know that she was being bullied there for being different.

At the age of thirteen, she wanted to shop exclusively in the boys' department. She would rather help her father with outside work than help me in the house. I couldn't understand why.

When she turned fourteen, we noticed that she was cutting herself, and suspected that she might be on drugs. We tried to get her help, but it seemed that every therapist, social worker, and psychologist we consulted said basically the same thing to us: "I can't help her; try this other person, _____." By the time she was sixteen, my daughter had seen over twenty different clinicians. This all took place in the 1970s, and no one knew about transgender issues back then, or understood how to work with my daughter and the many issues she was facing. We could barely understand then that my daughter was coming out as a lesbian. In fact, Tony is a twin, and his twin also came out as gay during those high school years.

On top of this, we didn't realize that Tony's twin was also grappling with feeling transgender. They both have now transitioned from female to male. Tony transitioned first, followed by his twin several years later. It has been easier to understand his twin's transition, because we had already gone through this with Tony.

It was very hard at first for me to accept that my child was transgender. This was mostly because I did not know how I was going to tell my husband. I did not know how to explain to him that our daughter was born in the wrong body. I didn't even know what *transgender* meant at first. And in fact, when I initially told my husband about it, he did not want to hear it at all, and we couldn't talk about it for a while.

Shortly after Tony shared the news with us that he was transitioning from female to male, I happened to watch a television show about a man who became a woman. Even though Tony's transition would be different, this show helped me begin to understand what it meant to be transgender.

I am sorry now that I didn't realize what was happening to my child when he was younger, and that I did not look into it further. It took me a while to understand it, but once I did, it all made sense—his childhood issues, the cutting, and his drug use. These were cries for help and for understanding which were not adequately addressed at the time.

Our child's transition has been sometimes hard to explain to other people, especially since my child still lives in our hometown. He is an activist here and very masculine in appearance. Even before hormone therapy, he actually already looked very much like a man. He has always been able to grow facial hair, and has had an unusually deep voice since he was young. After he began to take testosterone, he grew out his facial hair into a beard, and his voice deepened even more. He had his breasts removed and had a hysterectomy a few years later. I try to explain to people that he was born in the wrong body and that I support him by trying to get him help. I can only hope this assists people in better understanding what my son has gone through.

Our relationship with our son is very good now after a rough few years. Initially, it was hard not to wonder whether we had done something wrong. We had to learn many new things, such as using his new name rather than his birth name, and using the male pronoun when referring to him. This was very hard to do when speaking about someone I had raised as a daughter. And to be honest, sometimes I still slip with the wrong name or pronoun. I thank my son for giving me time to adapt to these changes.

It has also taken time to learn how to respond to other people's comments and questions, which were initially disconcerting. I once shared something with Tony that we are now able to laugh about today—but at the time it wasn't funny. Someone we know who was not accepting of Tony's transition asked me, "So you actually go to his house and visit him?" I was stunned, and in that moment realized exactly how hateful some people could feel about my child. My reply to that person was, "Of course I visit him, and of course I let him in my house. I love him, he's my daughter."

At this point, I feel we have accepted his transition and understand much more about transgender issues. And we love him for who he is. We are very proud of him, and of what he is doing for other transgender people. He has started support groups in our city for transgender teenagers, and one for their parents, as well as an art class for transgender and gender nonconforming children under the age of twelve. He has gone back to school and is now a certified life coach. His specialty is working with parents of transgender children, and he is working hard to help parents better understand and support their children. He recently won a statewide award in Connecticut for his work with transgender people. We are very proud of the struggles he went through to get where he is today. We know he is happy with his life now, and hope he will continue to be in the future.

Ann Ferraiolo lives in New Haven, Connecticut with her husband. She enjoys spending time with her new son and other members of her extended Italian family.

Am I Doing the Right Thing?

Jennifer L. Kahler

Am I doing the right thing? This is the question I ask myself each day, this is the question that I have asked myself numerous times as my son grew up, and this is the question that haunts me. My son, shortly after turning ten, transitioned into my daughter. Jack turned into Jackie, and as our family, school, and friends adjust to the new identity, I find myself constantly questioning my choices, my parenting, and the information that I have compiled. This would be so much easier with a manual and snapshot of the future.

This journey began when Jack was only two years old. From that age on, Jack liked all things feminine and all things pink. Jack was fascinated with Barbie dolls, princesses, mermaids, gowns, long hair, and dressing up. Jack used to put wigs on and wrap towels on his head, saying, "I punzel...this my long, long hair." He was constantly undressing and putting on tutus, boas, sparkle shoes, tiaras, and dress-up gowns. He once wore his sister's flower girl dress for days, and even insisted on sleeping in it.

Jack was given plenty of boys' toys, like trucks, Legos, superhero dolls, and Matchbox cars, but he never had any interest in playing with any of them. He wouldn't stand to pee, and he was often embarrassed about being "topless" at public pools. If he colored a picture, he always picked a princess or a mermaid. If he chose a balloon color, it was always pink. Every Halloween he wanted to be a princess or a ballerina. For his birthdays he always wanted dolls for gifts and a girly birthday cake. When we went to McDonald's, he always wanted the girls' toy in the Happy Meal. He always had friends that were girls, and always seemed to wish he, too, was a girl. Jack was more "girly" than any biological girl I had ever known. My husband, daughter and I gave up fighting Jack's girliness early on. It was just so natural for him and there was no stopping it.

When Jack was three, he asked me why God had made him a boy. Because we were in Wal-mart at the time, I hushed him up quickly. By then, I knew there was something different about Jack, and I began looking into the possiblity that he might be transgender. Over the past seven years, I kept hoping that this was a "phase," or that Jack would just end up gay. In my mind, I kept repeating, "*Please* not that, *please* not that..."

We tried to encourage Jack to play with *all* toys, advising him that he should broaden his play to include toy cars, sports, and other gender-neutral activities such as play dough, drawing, and music. This never worked. We even tried to tell him that the "Barbie fairy" came and took all the dolls away to give to other children. This didn't work, either.

Christmas and birthdays were particularly hard. Our family was supportive at first: "How cute, he likes dolls...I bet he'll be a great daddy one day." But as Jack got older, his doll playing and tastes in toys drew quite a bit of unwanted negative attention from both family and friends. He seemed absolutely obsessed with dolls, much more than our daughter, much more into them than I ever was.

I remember the first time Jack visited Santa, and he was so scared to tell Santa that he wanted a Barbie doll for Christmas. He looked back at me and was about to cry. Santa asked Jack, "How about a football?" Jack just nodded sadly, and I almost cried. I knew what Jack wanted and already, he was embarrassed and afraid to tell other adults.

Birthdays were just as difficult. Jack had only one birthday party with classmates, and that was when he was in kindergarten. He told the kids at school that he wanted Barbies and Bratz dolls. He did get two Bratz dolls, both from boys in his class, but both Bratz dolls were boys. At that age, he didn't hide his disappointment with gifts well. He never wanted another birthday party again.

One week after Jack's tenth birthday, he came to me and told me that he wanted to be a girl and that he couldn't be a boy anymore. I wasn't really shocked at the revelation, but I had little knowledge and direction. My first step was to get educated and try to make some supportive connections. I am a lawyer, and my husband is a lawyer who also holds a degree in psychology. So it seemed right to begin by researching the subject. But the information was initially overwhelming and contradicting.

I had originally thought that we would have years to do a transition. That this might happen much later down the road. I was afraid for my son, his sister, and my practice. How would our community handle this? How would school handle this?

We started out slow, advising Jackie that she could dress how she wanted when at home and when we traveled, but that she would still be a "boy" at all other times. Once Jackie started wearing girls' clothes and embracing her transgender identity, the flood gates opened and there was no closing them. We quickly went from a few borrowed items from her sister, to a few items I bought for her on clearance for fun, to paying for a whole new wardrobe.

As the days went by, the transition seemed to get faster and stronger. Now Jack was having meltdowns in the morning when putting on the boys' clothes, experiencing panic attacks at school, and feeling depressed. We eventually decided to tell the school what was going on. They were extremely supportive. On February 14th, Jackie's class was told about the situation and Jack returned to school as Jackie.

I can't believe how well her classmates accepted this. She had a play-date the first weekend and an invitation to a slumber party the second. Wow! I kept waiting for the other shoe to drop, but it didn't. I am moved to tears each time I think of how caring, understanding, and supportive the people around us have been. I can't believe I underestimated others so much. I am very appreciative and humbled by the outpouring of kindness, concern, and support.

Telling family and friends happened on a need-to-know basis, and so far, most are very accepting. As I predicted, my father had a lot of concerns and skepticism, and still does; but so do I. The most accepting person for Jackie has been her sister, Sagan. Sagan has supported and loved her unconditionally. She has shared her clothes and bedroom. She was the one who told Jackie's class about the transition, and explained it to them in a way only another child could.

It feels like I am on an emotional roller-coaster. Personally, I credit myself with being a very open, liberal-thinking individual. I am not religious. I believe that sexuality and gender identity are established by birth—nature, not nurture. At the time that this happened, I was just beginning a change in the direction of my own life. I had come to the realization that I was tired of living my life according to the "rules" that other people have set for me and for society in general.

After years and years of focusing on my spouse, law practice, and children, I had begun to focus on myself and my needs and desires. I grew up in a middle-class family, in a medium-sized city, in an average neighborhood. I went to average schools and had an average life. I kept wondering why it took me until the age of forty-one until I began thinking about what I wanted from life and pursuing what made me happy. I have happily given and given to others, but have seemed to have lost my self-identity along the way. I decided to change the rules for myself and do what I wanted. It was time to focus on what made me happy as a person, and to love and accept those around me whom I cared for.

I think this is why I was able to accept Jackie's revelation more easily than other parents in my situation. Of course I want my child to be happy, but there are the costs, both physical and emotional, to consider. What does a reasonable parent do? How do I balance the immediate happiness of my child with the possibility that by promoting her happiness now, I may be irreversibly jeopardizing her future life and happiness?

My journey with my transgender child is bittersweet. I can see how happy my child is living as a female. I am confident that my child can have, and will have, a happy, successful life despite the gender incongruence. Our family is adjusting, but supportive. But I worry whether I am doing harm to the child I love by allowing her to transition so early in life. Will I do harm to her if I allow her to use blockers and hormone therapy, preventing the progression of her natural puberty and sexual orientation? So much is not known on this matter; so many of my questions have no answers. Would my child evolve into a happy, homosexual man without the interventions that I permit?

This is why I lose sleep each night, not because I am in denial, not that I can't accept my child, but because I am uneasy with my actions if they turn out to be detrimental. I am an attorney, and in thinking like an attorney, I know that some studies indicate there is a small chance that my child will desist in gender identity incongruence post-puberty. How can I support my child without taking unnecessary risks? If I don't take such risks now, do we later run the risks of depression, suicide, illicit drug use, or of her running away? I don't want any of those things for my child, so that is why I support her transition now. I refuse to allow my dearly loved child to suffer these harms.

Despite some reports I have seen regarding desistence, I still feel that allowing Jackie to transition now is the best option. She is happy and I have learned through our numerous, lengthy talks in the past two months that she has been waiting a long time for this opportunity. I fear that if she didn't get to transition now, the idea of social transition would be the "forbidden fruit" that she would hold in her mind as the be-all and end-all of her happiness. I tell her that we have been supportive and understanding about the transition, and we would be supportive and understanding of a transition back, if that was ever something she wanted. We have grown closer as a family and we continue to embrace this change and learn more. We will be going to our first Transhealth Conference in June, and Jackie will enjoy attending a camp for transchildren this summer.

We will keep our minds and eyes open. We will try to make the best decisions for our beloved child. Jackie's transition has also created a transition for our family and lifestyle. The transition is the catalyst for a new and better chapter for our family: we've decided to sell our home and relocate our residence. For years we have lived in a very small, conservative town. And we don't really fit in well here. We want to protect Jackie and we believe life for our family would be easier in a new, potentially larger, more progressive, city. It was hard for me initially to let my house go. I felt I worked so hard my whole life to get to the point where I had a big, beautiful, impressive home. I now embrace the changes in our lives that are accompanying Jackie's transition. My big house never made me happy—my family always has and always will.

The financial costs of a transgender child are overwhelming, which is another good reason to downsize our lives. I don't like discussing this with my children because I don't want Jackie to feel like it is all her fault. But we never factored in having to pay for therapy at $200 per session, plus puberty blockers which can cost between $4,500 and $15,000 per year for the medication alone. It is likely we will need to pay for an endocrinologist too, not to mention cross-hormone treatment. Not only do most insurances not pay for these services and prescriptions, but we have a high-deductible plan, thus we pay out-of-pocket for everything. Jackie is also dyslexic, color-blind, is far-sighted, sensory seeking, has ADD, and suffers from poor tracking, poor auditory processing, and visual integration and perception deficits. She has "splintered" skills, scoring extremely high in some areas and extremely low in others. These problems require additional time and money.

This journey seems to be easier for Jackie now that she has transitioned. The rest of us are trying to keep up. However, she was not *born* a girl and no matter what she does, this won't change. This is a very hard reality for my ten-year-old to accept. Her reality and life will never be ideal for her, whether she continues down the road of transgender or chooses something else. The path is not clear and will probably be full of surprises.

I hope that sharing my experience will give others a better idea of who we are, who our child is, and why we are in this situation. I feel that our family has benefited from the experiences of other transgender people from years gone by, and I hope that our experience can be shared for those yet to come.

Jennifer Kahler is the mother of a ten-year-old transgender-affirmed daughter and a thirteen-year-old daughter. She is an attorney and practices law with her husband in a small-town firm. The experience of having a transgender child has inspired Jennifer and her family to support and advocate for the rights of all people on the gender spectrum.

My Princess Boy: A Mom's Story Becomes an International Phenomenon

An Interview with Cheryl Kilodavis by Rachel Pepper

Dyson is still young, but his love of all things pink and frilly has captured worldwide attention through numerous television appearances, sparking much debate on the phenomenon of being a "princess boy," a term that Dyson coined himself.

According to his mother Cheryl, Dyson began gravitating towards all things pink, purple, and sparkly as soon as he could walk and talk. Since Dyson was the second of her sons, Cheryl says, "We thought we had the road map for raising a boy down at that point." However, his interest in dressing up in her clothes caught her off guard. She says, "We tried to redirect this interest; we thought this was what we were supposed to do. So I'd give him a truck to play with, but he'd go right back to wanting to play with my purse."

As Cheryl found, all the redirection was making Dyson unhappy. She had already told him that he couldn't be a princess because boys just could not be princesses. He looked right at her, she says, and told her "Well, I am a princess boy."

Then, when he was three-and-a-half, she took him and his older brother shopping for Halloween costumes. Dyson wanted to be Cinderella, and began yelling loudly in the store. As Cheryl tried to placate him, and other parents stared, Dyson screamed, "I want to be a princess for Halloween!" Finally, Dyson's older brother asked, "Mom, why can't you just let him be happy?" Says Cheryl now, "That was my wake up call."

Cheryl began keeping a journal of this time, frequently writing about why this journey of acceptance was so difficult. "I wondered why this was making me so uncomfortable. I asked myself, is this really going to harm anyone?"

This was not an easy time for her and her husband. "I had cultural and spiritual preconceived notions that were blocking me," Cheryl says. She did not know there were other parents also dealing with young boys who crossed gender lines. During this time, she says, "I honestly thought that I was alone with this issue."

Over the next year, Cheryl and her husband came to realize that their son's happiness was more important than what other people might think of his clothes or his behavior. So, they began to let him wear more feminine clothing, although, she says, "At first, I hid this from family. We kept it in the house. But it became harder and harder to hide."

Eventually, Cheryl and her husband decided as a family to support Dyson fully. As her husband said to her, "If we can support Dkobe [the couple's other son] as a soccer player, we can support this child too." The couple sent a letter to family and close friends, explaining that they were absolutely supportive of Dyson's differences, and that they hoped everyone else in their lives would be, too.

After this revelation, some family members told her to "seek help" for herself and her child. Others were initially more accepting, and still others have eventually come around in their thinking.

During this time, Cheryl's journal helped her make sense of what her family was going through. She began to make copies of these journals at a local copy shop, and eventually began to sell them online. As the book took off, a groundswell of demand necessitated a major publisher take over this task, and *My Princess Boy* found a home at Simon & Schuster.

Cheryl has found that societal acceptance has been hardest in her own African-American community. However, she also finds that among older African Americans, the support has been surprisingly high. "Most older people have known someone in their life who hasn't fit in traditional gender categories," she says, or may even remember times in their own lives when *they* didn't.

"I am always hearing stories," Cheryl says, "from folks who say 'I wish I hadn't been pressured to play football as a teenager,' or 'I wish I had had more options in life.' I think we are helping take some pressure off what it means to be a man and still be part of the African-American community." She admits it took her some time "to connect the dots" and realize her own son was one such young man. Now, her aim is "to get the world on board." At Dyson's school, copies of the book she wrote are readily available, and she has made one directive absolutely clear to his teachers and administrators: "Don't crush my son's spirit."

Because Dyson is still a child, it is hard to know where he will land on the gender spectrum when he grows up. Cheryl says she "has absolutely wondered" about what Dyson's gender identity and sexual orientation will be when he is older. Like many parents of gender nonconforming children, she and her husband have already made the rounds of pediatricians and child psychologists, and have settled on the advice "to just support him" where he is, talking about gender and sexuality with him as the need arises.

At five, Cheryl says, Dyson "feels ok about being a boy" even while living and dressing as a princess boy whenever he can. As he grows, Cheryl and her husband are prepared to "accept him for who he is, no matter what. We signed up as parents to be the best guides for him that we can be, not for us, but for him."

Cheryl feels strongly about the issue of full acceptance for any child, no matter the circumstances. "Exclusion hurts," she says. "We cannot have our children taking their own lives." Their family is now part of a wider web of support that includes all types of people, including families through adoption, LGBT families, and gender variant adults and children.

Cheryl is aware that through her book's amazing success, she has been thrown into the spotlight in unexpected ways. This has included numerous television appearances with Dyson, who is usually dressed in feminine attire for such occasions. However, Cheryl knows that going public has put a face to this issue for millions of people. "It has helped people understand this issue and also accept families like us." She currently receives hundreds of emails a week, mostly from families trying to make sense of their child, and of their own journeys of acceptance.

Of African American and Caucasian heritage, Cheryl grew up in Seattle, Washington. As a child, she used journal writing to answer life's questions such as why things were as they were and why people felt it was necessary and even okay, to judge others. Although never published until *Princess Boy* was released, Cheryl continued writing after marrying her high-school sweetheart with whom she had her two sons. She feels proud to be able to stand up for difference, and especially proud of her own Princess Boy, Dyson.

Cheryl Kilodavis is an advocate for families with gender nonconforming children and the author of **My Princess Boy,** *a book about her gender variant son,* **Dyson.**

Ceeb

Debi Russell

When Courtney was sixteen, she came to her dad and I and told us that she was a lesbian. Now at this point in her life, this did not surprise me—she had never been a foo-foo girl. At five years old, she had announced to us that she would never wear a dress again. As she grew, she wanted only boys' toys, including Micro Machines, model cars, and such.

As a mom, I felt Courtney was destined for something different, and that her life would not be easy or simple. She would have to struggle to be happy. Little did I know what a struggle that would actually be.

During her first year of college, Courtney came home for Christmas break and asked to talk to her dad and me alone. It was then that she told us that she wanted to transition to a male.

She was so concerned that we would throw her out the door that night that she had already made plans to stay with friends.

This announcement was more than a bit ironic. Just minutes before this happened, while we waited for her to get home, her dad and I wondered why she had called this meeting and I had jokingly said…the only thing she would want to talk to us about privately would be to change her sex!

After the initial shock—which felt a lot like a punch in the stomach—we talked about what exactly was entailed in doing what she wanted to do. She described the process ahead, the testosterone shots, the chest surgery, the change of name and sex on her records, the telling of family and friends. I told her that no matter what, we would love her and be there for her. Her dad hugged her and said he supported any decision she made. And so began my journey with Courtney, and with all the bumps in the road that are part of letting go of the little girl I gave birth to and embracing the young man she was about to become.

The months ahead were filled with heartache and tears. Not because I didn't want this for her, but because I knew this was going to be very hard for her. My biggest fear was that people would think she was a freak, and that broke my heart in two. The only thing I knew about transitioning was what I saw on *The Jerry Springer Show,* which is really no knowledge at all.

I honestly did not know where to turn. Thank goodness for the Internet, which helped me to connect with the right groups. I joined an online network, and the wonderful people there answered my questions, helped with my concerns, and gave me information with links to surgeons, doctors, drugs, and the like. I traveled to a weekend get-together of parents, and got to actually sit and talk to those who had gone through what I was going through. That helped lighten my load.

I joined the PFLAG group in our city and attended alone on a regular basis. Courtney's dad was not interested in going. He had decided to deal with her transition in his own way. After about a year, I stopped going myself. I was the only mom of a transgender child, and felt I was not really a part of the group. Courtney's dad and I did sit on several panels at workshops and talked about our "new son," Cianán, whom I call Ceeb.

Cianán is our oldest child. We have a daughter, Megan, who is nineteen months younger. She struggled the most with this transition and, for a time, said she would never call Courtney her brother. So we worked to show her that letting go of her sister would come with time. And it did. She is much closer to her brother now than she ever was with Courtney. Part of that is maturity, I realize, but seeing them with a better relationship has meant a lot to me.

Telling family and friends was not as tough as I expected. Those that could not accept this change—and there were some—we just let go from our lives. Our closest family members embraced Cianán with their hearts. Our real friends did the same and it was so heartwarming to feel the support. We needed that then. We needed to know those we cared about would not turn their backs on us.

Eight months after he talked to his dad and I, Cianán and I traveled to San Francisco where he had his chest surgery. This felt like a hugely important step for my child, as Courtney had large breasts, so large that strapping her chest was out of the question. Dr. Brownstein, the surgeon we employed, was wonderful, and we felt Cianán was in good hands. The surgery went well and we spent the next eight days in a hotel room while he recuperated. This was a good bonding time for us. I cannot express the pride I felt the first time I saw Cianán walk with his shoulders back, happy in his body.

I never once felt that this transition was a bad idea, or wrong, or out of the question. I had this beautiful baby given to me, and my one and only wish was for his happiness. The heartache I felt watching him the first eighteen years of his life was far more painful than letting the little girl go. Cianán is an inspiration to me. He is the bravest young man I know. And I am grateful I was there to help him along the way, and thankful beyond words that I still have him in my life.

Cianán has gone on to receive his PhD in Chemical Education. His transition took place ten years ago. He is now a happy, beautiful young man—beautiful inside and out. I could not be any prouder of him than I am today.

Debi Russell is sixty years old and has lived in the Kansas City area for over forty years. She has a twin sister, as well as an older brother and sister, and they are all very close. She recently received her real estate license after thirty-one years of being a homemaker. Also, after thirty-one years of marriage, she is now divorced. She loves to knit, read, bowl, travel, and cook in her spare time. Ceeb is the nickname she calls her child.

Kid Chrysalis

Amy Marsh

Some of what I know as a mother, particularly as the mother of a transgender child, was learned way back in my teens, when I began to live with and support my childhood sweetheart, John.

John's own mother kicked him out for six months when he was thirteen, and again, finally, at age fifteen. John's mother rejected him for being "effeminate," and queer. While he was on the streets, he did what most street kids do in order to eat and live—but I didn't understand that until later.

We were both students at a non-accredited hippie "free school." We met there and fell in love. After we joined a jobs program for underprivileged youth, we decided to live together. Our combined income of about $300 a month allowed us to rent a one-bedroom apartment in a rundown, coastal town.

Being young and vegetarian we didn't think about other practicalities, such as eating. We were young and in love and this was many years ago.

This was the beginning of a long period of trauma in my life, as John's suicide attempts, thievery, and chaotic liaisons with his "tricks" began to disrupt the sweet, childlike relationship we'd originally concocted together—something mostly sexless and quite unlike the other realities of his life. At nineteen, John took himself into a canyon with a bunch of pills and never came out again. And I was beside myself with grief...and relief. It was finally my time to emerge from a deep well of confusion and find out for myself what life was all about. The normal milestones for young adults, including high school graduation and college, had passed me by. I've spent a lot of time since then trying to approximate those milestones, though at wildly unusual times of life.

With such a background, you'd expect me to go overboard in providing protection, stability, and unconditional love for my own children. As a mother, that's pretty much what I've done, though still in the context of a somewhat bohemian life.

Prior to marriage and pregnancy, I spent my time in creative projects: making wearable art and producing alternative fashion shows, co-founding a nonprofit organization to promote women's involvement in outer space exploration, and singing in a new wave band, while also working meaningless day jobs. Eventually, I helped my husband start the business that supports us to this day.

At age thirty-six, I was mentally ready for children, but my body had different plans. Some pre-term labor resulted in eleven weeks of strict bed rest. Luckily, medical intervention worked. The baby was born healthy and full-term, apparently a girl.

This child was very alert, wakeful, demanding. You could almost see the baby brain at work, putting it all together. We knew *she* was an extraordinary being. Yes, most parents think this and it's true for everyone's child, but this was *our* kid, and we experienced this child as an extraordinary gift in our lives.

Oddly, when I held my newborn in my arms, I was mostly struck by the incredible courage of the incarnating soul. To fling oneself into the waiting arms of a stranger, so much bigger and potentially capable of destruction as well as love, seemed valiant as well as foolhardy. So my baby's courage and trust made an indelible impression. I knew I would never betray her.

During my pregnancy, I had also tumbled into chronic environmental illness and chemical sensitivity. During those first years with my child, I was often ill. I couldn't handle extended forays into the outside world. So I stayed at home with my child and entered once again into the world of child-hood, giving the highest priority to enriching that world with books, toys, color, festivals, and love, in a way that echoed my earlier involvement with John. These were uneasy memories, and I mostly pushed them away. I immersed myself in discovering this new being, my child, as "she" discovered the world.

Seven years later, our second child was born, this time a boy. For both kids, early childhood consisted of co-op nursery schools, the Waldorf School, holiday celebrations, music, art, and lots of trips to natural history museums and parks. By this time I had learned to manage my illness, and paced my daily activities based on the likelihood of toxic exposures. In this way, I was able to make good use of everything San Francisco could offer a family. We were happily raising a brilliant, artistic daughter (so we thought) and a wonderfully spirited boy.

However there were stresses and strains. I had a chronic illness and so my husband was the sole support for the family. Asher, our oldest child, was never really "happy," in spite of all we did, and our youngest, well, we did what we could to keep life pleasant for all concerned. The two kids never really clicked with each other—they were so far apart in age. For years it was like raising two children who were both an "only child."

Asher was outwardly very much a girl. He liked girls' things, but he also had quirky interests and didn't really care to socialize in a girly way. Squealing and fawning over a budding queen bee was of no interest at all. He was smart and he was shy. He had friends of all genders, but often seemed somewhat alone. As he grew older and came closer to puberty, his social ostracism was more pronounced. This was partly the work of a "mean girl" in his class, but also, in hindsight, indicative of his dawning alienation from what we expected him to be.

I was relieved when we moved and Asher changed schools. This gave him a fresh start, new friends, and an extraordinary teacher from sixth to eighth grade. By eighth grade, he had come out as bisexual. By tenth grade, he was sick of being one of two openly queer kids in a small high school and was struggling with his assigned gender. For a long time, we knew nothing of the latter, though we strongly supported him in his sexual identity. By this time, I saw my experiences with John as a gift. His memory enabled me to be completely and proudly supportive of Asher.

I realize now that if Asher had been identifiable as transgender at a young age, life would have been easier for him.

He would not have felt "neglected"—as he put it—because he would have been seen and recognized for who he is. Probably many features of his childhood would have stayed the same— the Waldorf School, harp lessons, acting—but he would have been spared the changes at puberty which were secretly repugnant to him. We truly didn't know what he was going through. We thought we had a bright, brave, and eccentric daughter. What we really had was a bright, brave, and eccentric older son.

As Asher struggled with his own development and identity, I experienced my own middle-aged "coming out" as a polyamorous person. Unfortunately, our attempt at an "open marriage" was unsuccessful, and our family began to unravel and morph into something less acceptable to many other families in our community. I also went back to school to study human sexuality, and gained an intellectual framework for sexual and gender diversity which has helped me deal with past and present emotional challenges.

In his eighteenth year, Asher was raped and assaulted while still presenting as female. I cannot express the anguish and rage I still feel about this. After the rape, I watched my child disintegrate before my eyes. Asher was frequently suicidal. There was a time when we might have lost him. That this was happening to Asher at the same age that John committed suicide added to my terror. (Asher has published an account of this, so I am not breeching his confidentiality.) Though Asher's thoughts of suicide have mostly subsided, the assault left him with post-traumatic stress and frequent anxiety.

Some months later, Asher told us of his desire to transition to male. I was surprised, but it also made sense. I'm not saying this was exactly easy to hear, but it became apparent to all of us that Asher's claiming of his true self saved his life. Our acceptance—and testosterone—support him in his authenticity. His younger brother prefers Asher as an older brother and their relationship is better than ever. As a young man, Asher now has greater confidence, a wide circle of friends, a wonderful primary relationship, and attends college. I am proud of his courage, clarity, and outspoken activism. And while he suffers residual trauma, I feel that he is growing in strength and has the capacity to transmute and transcend it.

At first, I sometimes missed the "girl child," but that seldom happens now. I now see the artificial assignment of gendered persona as a chrysalis, which supported the true being of my child in prolonged incubation, until Asher himself could emerge and spread his bright, dark wings. As a mother, I am honored to behold the power and beauty of my child's authentic self. Because of Asher, and because of John, I am a passionate advocate for a world where all children can claim their authentic gender and sexual expression, without parental rejection and violence.

Amy Marsh is a clinical sexologist and hypnotherapist with a doctorate in human sexuality. She is a mother of two. She wrote weekly for Carnal Nation, and currently writes sexuality blogs and does internet radio. She advocates for sexual social justice, Hawaiian sovereignty, and disability rights, and also volunteers on a suicide crisis line.

Transfamily

Michelle Schnur

My transgender child is currently nineteen years of age and the happiest he's ever been. Born female with no birthing complications, she had all the normal body parts and was healthy. A girl was just what I wanted, since we already had a son and were not planning on having any other children. We named her Heather Elizabeth.

My husband and I had an understanding that I would be a stay-at-home mom for our youngest, but unfortunately for me, my husband got laid off from his job and I had to return to full-time work. Luckily, Heather still had a stay-at-home parent, and she and her dad have always had a very strong bond. I refer to them as two peas in a pod.

Heather was doted on by all, and was especially blessed to

have an older brother, almost ten years her senior, who adored her. By age three, it was evident that Heather was drawn to, and favored, the male figures in her world.

A key turning point in our lives occurred when Heather was between the ages of three and four. I am not a girly-girl myself and rarely wore dresses, so it seemed natural that she'd lean toward a more boyish style. But she adamantly informed us that she did not want to wear dresses or anything girl-like at all, even on special holidays. Stubbornness was a trait that she came by honestly, but this was different.

Heather played with a variety of toys, including dolls and character figures. We always said she was in love with John Smith from the Disney cartoon *Pocahontas*. But looking back, I now think that she identified with him as a male figure. Many times on family vacations she would ask us to call her by a boys' name that she was fond of at the time, and we would play along.

In her early school years, she had both boy and girl friends, but her best friends were always boys. She enjoyed making the sound of bodily noises for fun, she loved the outdoors, and she loved swimming and biking. She dabbled in sports, but did not like to be obliged to stick with them. Again, looking back, I think she tried them out because that was what the other boys liked to do.

By the time Heather was eight, her hair was cut short and we were shopping exclusively in the boys' department for her. And she gave up swimming because she had to wear a girls' swimsuit. The only girl item I drew the line on was underwear. I insisted she still had to wear girls' underwear. I don't know why. She dressed like a boy on the outside, so what difference did it make what kind of underwear she wore? Perhaps

I thought it was the only way of holding onto the daughter I knew I had.

I was beginning to struggle with the whole idea of this being only a "phase." Family members, friends, and teachers all told me not to worry, that she was just a tomboy. But I didn't think she was a tomboy, since, for one thing, she didn't really like to play or watch sports.

By eleven, Heather's breasts were developing, and by twelve she had her first menstruation. These years were so dark for her; she was absolutely devastated when she started developing breasts and had to wear a bra. She started wearing loose fitting clothes to hide her bumps and curves. She talked of death often and wore only black clothes. Menstruation was something she could not ignore, although she tried. She began perceiving me as an enemy because I was the one that told her she was a biological girl and that this was something she had to deal with. A deep depression set in, and we needed to seek outside help from professionals. By this time, I had even given in about the underwear. It was evident that she was indeed transgender.

Our family was familiar with gender-related issues. My husband revealed to me before we were married that he was a cross-dresser. Although I did not understand his belief that it was just about the clothes, I decided it was a small compromise.

As the years rolled by, my husband's occasional cross-dressing evolved into a much bigger issue. It had become a reoccurring sore spot in our marriage. He spent much of his time and resources striving to look like a woman, but always denied to me that he wanted to be a woman. At one point, he decided he wanted to be able to dress as he liked around the house. That is when our children were informed that he was a cross-dresser and that he was going to be free to dress in women's clothing whenever he felt like it.

It was that same year that our oldest son began having anger issues. When this son was seventeen, he went to basic training for the National Guard, and after that summer, he came back to us a different soul. More angry and cold and closed-off than ever. He started drinking alcohol, abusing drugs, committing crimes, and spent the next decade in and out of prison. We tried getting him help on many occasions, but had no success. After returning from his first sentence in state prison, he announced to me that he was bisexual. I had had no idea, but it did not matter to me. I just wanted him to be happy and that is what I told him.

On our fifteenth wedding anniversary, my husband confessed that he had finally come to terms with his true identity. He said that he was meant to be a woman, and would begin to pursue transitioning. I wanted to be understanding, and I felt I did understand the transgender thing as I had read many books on the subject through the years, but it felt like a betrayal, as well.

All these years he insisted it wasn't going to come to this. I was hurt, I was angry, I was devastated! My whole world was going to change, and all our hopes and dreams together were no longer relevant. He had new hopes and dreams that he needed to pursue to be his true self. I was grieving: I had lost a husband, and I had lost my way of life.

During this difficult time, our family structure was crumbling and we were all in therapy, except for my oldest son, who was in prison. My husband wanted our twelve-year-old daughter Heather to go through transition with him, including surgery. We changed child therapists a number of times because he wanted to find one who would agree to this for Heather, and none of them would. The professional opinion (which I shared) was that it would be best to wait until Heather was over puberty before any drastic measures such as surgery were taken. This decision only created a bigger wedge between me and my husband and child. It was heartbreaking all around.

At the age of sixteen, Heather legally changed her name to Damon Joseph and started hormone treatments of testosterone. At eighteen, Damon underwent peri-areolar (purse-string) mastopexy, a type of mastectomy to remove his breasts. Since then he has started to wear more appropriate fitting clothing and has added more color to his wardrobe.

Damon and I have become closer over the last few years, and I don't believe that he holds any grudges towards me. He knows I love him and that my decisions were made out of love and concern for his well-being. Actually, for the most part, as a family we always let Damon be who he was comfortable being. He is a happy, well-adjusted adult, and I am very proud of him. Most of the negative stress and adversity during Damon's transition came from teachers and peers, and gaining the community's understanding and acceptance is still a challenge for him.

The last decade has been a most difficult one for me, and besides adapting to my youngest being transgender, I've had to deal with many other major life issues over these years. During this time, my father died of brain cancer, I had to have a complete hysterectomy, and I began having panic attacks. I decided that I was not able to live with my husband as a woman and moved out of our home. Then I was diagnosed with breast cancer and had to have a mastectomy followed by chemotherapy and radiation, followed by reconstructive surgery.

When it comes to my husband, I still have a lot of mixed feelings. It has been a most difficult separation. As for my oldest son, he has had a few romantic relationships with men. As far as I can tell he's not interested in women. He is currently serving his fifth year in state prison. As always, I hope and pray that he will be able to come to terms with his issues and turn his life around for good.

It has been a slow process for me, creating new hopes and dreams, and finding a new, purposeful direction for my life. I thank God every day for all my blessings and look forward to the best future for my family.

Michelle A. Schnur is a native of western Pennsylvania, the mother of two children and a breast cancer survivor who co-founded the support group Family & Friends of Inmates. She is also an advocate and member of her local chapter of PFLAG.

Camp I Am

Diana Wilson

My son, who is a self-described "half girl, half boy," was extremely hesitant to join in on the first evening of Camp I Am. Camp I Am is a parent-organized, volunteer-run camp for male-born, gender nonconforming and transgender children, as well as their families, who are connected through a listserv at the Children's National Medical Center. My son didn't know what to expect and felt incredibly nervous, which is common for him when faced with any new setting.

I, on the other hand, was very eager to participate after five years of being on the listserv and reading about families coming to the camp from afar. Now it was our turn to be part of this unique experience. We took the plunge, and travelled from Tucson to a remote camp in New Hampshire to meet the families and their wonderfully expressive children. The rest is full of blissful, incredible memories that our family will never forget. There were icebreakers, dance parties, arts and crafts, a seamstress to make dresses at a moment's notice, and, of course, campfires and s'mores at night to end each joy-filled, exhausting day. It was, in short, Utopia.

I have never seen my child so free, so unencumbered by his frequent self-censoring anxiety. Here he knew he could wear a dress any time of the day or night without having to stop and think about who might see him, who might judge him, or who might say something hurtful. He embraced the fashion show and walked the runway—more than once, I might add—with a confidence that is usually reserved for his at-home nightly musical theater shows. He then spent the next hour or two dancing in the music-filled hall with complete abandon. It was powerful stuff that brought me to tears more than once.

At Camp I Am, children do the same kinds of activities that any kid going to camp might experience. However, this is all done in an environment that felt safe all day long for our kids, kids who often don't feel safe expressing who they are.

Like all of us parents of gender-creative children, my husband and I didn't sign up for this life. And we don't have a crystal ball to tell us exactly why our son has so many feminine traits. We didn't think much of it when he was a toddler and would choose to dress up in skirts, put on my jewelry, and dance around the room with a smile. We didn't worry when he would shun any sort of organized sports in favor of playing with dolls or dressing up around the house. We also didn't make a big deal of it when he wanted to wear a dress to his preschool, and no one there blinked an eye, either. It never occurred to us not to support our son in his self-expression, and we've been fortunate to live in a community of friends who don't judge us for that.

Of course, our son now knows, simply by looking around at other children, that he is unique in his gender expression. Now that he's not a young child, he sees examples everywhere that indicate that he is quite different. This can induce stress in a child as they grow and yearn to fit in, to be part of the crowd.

I have read the comments on like-minded parents' blogs, and I know there are many people out there who think we are completely nuts, or that we're setting our child up for a disastrous outcome. I am not naïve enough to think that my son won't have some big challenges down the road, which is why he sees a wonderful psychologist who will work with us through these years of gender ambiguity. We take each day as it comes, but mostly we want our son to grow up confident and proud of who he is, whomever that turns out to be.

And now he is eight. Early childhood has ended with a crash and the game has changed. He knows he is different. This past summer, he has talked at times about "turning into a girl"; he thinks it would be easier to be a girl than to remain a "boy who likes girl stuff." It's heartbreaking. Lately though, after seven months of growing his hair longer, he has mentioned that maybe he will just "be a boy with long hair." We are left wondering if this is his true self or the result of pressure to conform to the world around him. But, he has never expressed discomfort with his body, and we take this as a sign that he is simply gender fluid, at least for now.

I don't get to skip ahead to the last page of this story, and while it is extremely difficult sometimes, I accept it. I try to remind myself what an amazing gift life has given me. I have learned about patience, unconditional love, bravery, and acceptance, but most of all, I have realized that I am not in charge of my son's destiny. I am here to take his lead and support him in the best way I can.

The last night of camp was a talent show where kids performed skits, played instruments, told stories, sang or lip-synched songs, or acted just plain goofy. The latter would certainly describe my son! It was the kids' time to shine and be embraced, and at the end, when we danced as a big group to Lady Gaga's *Born This Way*, even little brother, who is "all boy" and quite introverted, couldn't resist the urge to get up and boogie. When it was over, we were all exhausted but elated.

After camp, my son mentioned to me that he wished his school could be just like Camp I Am. I took this to mean that he wished he would never have to monitor what he chose to wear or what he played with, and that girls and boys would play together without anyone imposing gender norms.

It hurts when the girls at school shun him in favor of "girls-only" play. He often sees himself as one of them. Of course, they don't understand that. But we are fortunate to be at a small Montessori charter school where the teachers "get it" about our "pink boy" and do all they can to make sure he feels safe. It's inherent in the virtues they teach to the students each week as part of the curriculum: acceptance, honor, friendliness, compassion, kindness, justice, and respect. They have also read the children's books *My Princess Boy* and *10,000 Dresses* to his class, with my son proudly sitting next to his teacher. Afterwards, they had a great discussion about differences and how each child is unique, and that we can all work to accept each other and celebrate those differences. He has truly blossomed there, and we will continue to work with the staff to ensure they understand our child's unique social challenges as he gets older.

After hearing so many stories about fathers resistant to accepting a gender nonconforming child or their own child's gender creativity, I am all the more grateful to have a husband who works with me to learn about and embrace our son for who he is. Perhaps it is due in part to his European upbringing and his worldwide travels, along with the fact that he is a child psychologist. No matter where my husband learned it, I know our son benefits greatly from having a male role model who practices non-judgment and unconditional acceptance of others. Camp I Am, he says, was a turning point for him. He has always gone along with my son's interests, but now he demonstrates his acceptance by telling him how beautiful he looks in a dress-up outfit, or reminding him of how important it is for him to be true to himself. I know this makes a difference and will matter all the more as our child grows older.

As we were saying our goodbyes at this year's camp, we started to plan our road trip to camp for the next year. As for me, I think it's time to start planning a southwestern version of Camp I Am closer to home for families who may not be able to travel so far. Don't all our unique children deserve to have an experience like we did?

Diana Wilson is a mom with an amazing husband and two kids in Tucson, AZ, who is passionate about supporting not only her own gender nonconforming son, but all children who express gender differently than the "norm" in our binary culture. She works in higher education student development and counseling and teaches courses on student success and career exploration.

To My Child

Geraldine Boothe

Dearest Ruby (or Will),

It's 1:44 a.m., and I can't sleep. Tonight I got mad at Ann and decided to crash in your room. I was tired, and I wanted to go to bed early. You took the top bunk, and I the bottom. We had several false starts. First you needed water—in a thermos. Then your fingernails were bothering you, so I found the tiny scissors. The lights went out, and it was time to sing "Hukilau."

We talked for a while. You wanted to know my favorite number. It's twenty-four; yours is twelve. I asked you what some of your favorite days were. You replied, meeting my partner Ann and her dog, Simba, going to sleepaway camp for a week, being at school, and visiting Disneyland. Some of mine were seeing my thirty-five-year-old sister graduate from college, getting the keys to my house, finding out I was pregnant, the day you were born, and meeting Ann (and Simba). I asked you what you would want if a fairy godmother could grant you any wish. You said you wanted to be a boy who could change into a dog or a mouse. I didn't say anything.

I think about you all the time. Parents worry a lot, at least I do. Eye infections, ear infections, toilet training, constipation, chronic strep throat, learning how to carry the one in addition—these were some of the challenges that have come and gone. Now, there's something new, something the parenting books don't cover. This past summer, at age eight-and-a-half, you told me for the first time that you wanted to be a boy. You have wanted to be a lot of things—a pirate, a writer, an illustrator, Aang the Avatar, a dog, and a mouse—so being a boy seemed like one more persona to try on.

A few days after the first time you disclosed your wish to be a boy, you asked for boys' underwear. I felt very uncomfortable and taken aback—why exactly did you want *boys'* underpants. I tried to play it cool, and I lied: "Sweetpea, I just bought you lots of new underwear on sale, and we can't return them. Let's wait until you grow out of these." You accepted that explanation.

A friend had co-authored the book, *The Transgender Child*. When I started reading it, I did so to support the author. Soon, I was reading it for us. Puzzle pieces started to form a different picture than I expected. All your stuffed animals have boys' names. Your baby doll is a boy. You want to wear a tuxedo if Ann and I get married. You asked for a boys' bathing suit last summer, which you got and wore with a matching swim shirt.

We cut your hair short—you hate your curlies. But you wanted a *real* boys' cut, like your friend José's. You used the scissors at school to snip off even more hair. You've been Peter Pan and the Avatar for the last two Halloweens, and boy animal characters before that. Every time you and your friends play a pretend game, you are a boy. I was proud that you didn't embrace typical girl things like Barbies or dressing up as a princess. You were a tomboy! But were you a girl making these bold choices, or a boy asserting himself?

The more I learned about transkids, the more I grilled you, every day. I'm ashamed of my relentlessness, but I had to know.

"Why do you want to be a boy?"

"I don't know."

"You know, girls can do anything boys can do. The only difference is that boys have a penis, and girls have a vagina and can have babies when they grow up."

(No response.)

"How long have you wanted to be a boy?"

"Since kindergarten." (Wow, I didn't know. You've been holding on to this desire for a long time—almost three years.)

"Do you want to *be* a boy, or do you *feel* like a boy?"

"Huh? What's the difference?"

"When you grow up, do you want to be a man or a woman?"

"A man."

"You wouldn't be able to have babies, but you could always adopt kids."

"Okay."

When Ann and I are alone, this is all I can talk about.

I obsess. And I agonize, and I cry. I scour the Internet. I've started going to a support group.

When we took our last vacation, we let you be a boy. No one knew you, so what could be the harm. You took your pierced earrings out, for good, it seems. We called you "Will," the name I would have given you if you'd been born a boy. When we returned home, you went through your closet and got rid of all your dresses (well, actually I saved two that I really liked, just in case), anything pink, and anything tight (like girls' shirts).

"*Why* did you have to give me a girly name?" you asked.

"Huh?" I never thought a gender neutral name would be necessary.

I told you about the *No Bikini* short that Ann and I had seen at the Lesbian & Gay Film Festival. In it, a little girl and her mom go shopping for a bathing suit. All they can find is a bikini, and every time the girl lifts her arms, the top rides up and her flat chest shows. Her mom says, "You're going to have to watch that." The girl goes by herself to her first swimming lesson and changes into her suit. That top isn't working. So, she makes a decision. She leaves the dressing room wearing only the bottoms. Her name is Robin, and her hair is shoulder length. The kids and teacher think she is a boy. For the whole summer, she passes. In the last scene she's in the car with her mother who is reading the teacher's notes: "Robin has really improved *his* strokes...." The mother is so puzzled, and Robin smiles to herself in the back seat of the car. You *love* this story.

The next time we went to the pool, *you* wanted to swim without *your* shirt. I was really nervous, so I put you off by saying you'd get sunburned. Then I told you I was worried your friends would tease you. "Mom, they won't recognize me," you said. I raised my eyebrows. You told me, "Besides, everybody knows I want to be a boy." They do? Selfishly, I'm worried about what their parents will say. Finally, I thought, what the hell. For the last five minutes, I let you go shirtless. What a huge smile you gave me as you leapt off the high dive.

The dominos keep falling over. You want to start using the men's bathrooms. I use them all the time when the women's rooms are full; it's no biggie. As long as it's a single stall in a place we know, like our favorite restaurant, it's okay by me. I don't want you to think you can always use the men's room. I worry something bad will happen, like you'll get molested, or found out and beaten or raped. But of course, I don't say this to an eight-year-old. I did say, "You can't use the boys' bathroom at school. They think you're a girl, and you will get in trouble." I wanted to see if you would push back, and maybe tell me you can't go into the girls' restroom because you *are* a boy. You didn't, my compliant child—or maybe my girl who likes pretending to be a boy.

Some people who go to our church are transgender. One transwoman is also named Ruby. We've met her a few times, and recently we bumped into her at the bookstore. I struggled whether to tell you about transgender people—what sorts of ideas will that give you? If I'd known about gay people when I was younger, I would have come out earlier, and probably without so much self-hatred about being different. I finally can't withhold this information, so I told you that our adult friend Ruby was born a boy. You were surprised and wanted to know how she changed. I don't know a lot about transgender people, but I told you they take drugs (good ones) to become the other gender. Grown-up Ruby might have had surgery to make breasts or change her penis into a vagina. Then, to be absolutely clear, I let you know that women can become men, too.

I feel guilty. I don't understand why this is happening, and somehow I feel it's got to be my fault. I have a meeting with one of the leaders of the local transkid parent support group, and she lets me off the hook. I realize that you don't want to be a boy because I'm a lesbian, or because I had you as a single mom, or because I took fertility drugs. It's not because I didn't fill your life with male role models, or because I expected you to be a boy even though I really wanted a girl, and now I'm being punished. This isn't about me or what I did wrong: it just is.

Sometimes I try to cling to the girl parts I do know. You like playing on girls' sports teams, and all your close friends are girls. You love Laura Ingalls Wilder's *Little House* books, and you play with baby dolls and barely touch that expensive train set your Grammy gave you. I know, I'm grasping at stereotypes. And, as much as I want your being a boy to be a fun fantasy, I feel in my gut there's more to it.

Even though Ann and I have only known about your desire to be a boy for a few months, you've known for over three years. I have to take you seriously. I love you to pieces, and I always will. Will, I'm scared where this gender change could take you: teased by mean kids, getting beat-up by bullies, not having a date for the prom, being discriminated against. We are going down a thickly tangled and barely travelled path, and I'm trying to step out in front and hack down the more noxious weeds before you get there. But you are excited by the things you glimpse, and you rush ahead with joyful abandon. In these short months, I have met other truly wonderful and brave parents and children. You are helping me grow into a better person. I will do whatever I can to support you in being your authentic self, but sometimes that won't be easy for me, and sometimes I'll do or say stupid things. But I'll always love you.

I will give you this letter when you're grown up, so you'll know how your story started. I'm worried about the choices we may or may not make, and I want you to know the decisions have come after lots of struggle and from a deep love for you. You're still only a child, and for now, I'm going to try and let you be. You have time before you need to think about puberty blockers, bathrooms, names, changing schools, junior high locker rooms, high school locker rooms, finding a partner, fertility…I will hold these fears for now. And, in the meantime, as my gay, lesbian, and straight forefathers and foremothers did for me, I will try to make our community a better place for all transgender people.

It's 3:57 a.m., and I finally feel very tired. My nose is stuffy—I've been crying. Your hand hangs over the top bunk, and I kiss it.

Love, love, love,
Mama

Geraldine Boothe (pseudonym) wrote "To My Child" three years ago. Her daughter Ruby is now her son Will, age eleven-and-a-half. They enjoy living in the progressive Bay Area with their awesome dog, Toph Bei Fong, surrounded by loving friends and family.

Still the Same Soul

Rebecca Lewis

Several years ago my daughter, an artist in her twenties, drew an interesting picture. The picture was of her, face-to face with a young man that could have been her twin.

Soon after this, we were driving together, and she seemed tense and worried. She said that she was thinking of herself as a man, but she wasn't sure what that meant and wondered if she should transition to look like a man.

Being an older parent in my late fifties who was not really up on things, I had no idea what she was talking about. My daughter had been bisexual for years, but had never mentioned anything about being a man. I just listened, and was totally surprised and amazed as she described what she was thinking of doing. She was thinking of taking testosterone. I asked if she was thinking of surgery, and she said, "No." I did have an acquaintance whom I had known as a man, but who had transitioned to look like a woman. She seemed happy and at home when I met her again in a women's choir. This was my only experience with any person who had transitioned to look like another sex.

Over the next few months we talked more about this idea, and my daughter gave my husband and me a book to read by a transgender man. After reading the book, I became more and more afraid for the safety of my child. Gays, lesbians, and bisexuals were often targets for hate and the victims of hate crimes, and transgender people were no exception.

I found myself having many questions about what transitioning would mean for my child, especially as he was now an adult and potentially would have to interact with less tolerant people than he had in college. Would he be able to get a job? Would he be safe? Would he be able to meet good people and form loving, long-term relationships? And what were the long-term effects of testosterone on a female body?

My daughter was a grown person who could make her own decisions and take responsibility for them. I was afraid of possible consequences, but I had to let go and give these fears over to God, the spirit of all life. And I surrendered my fears for her again and again.

As I attempted to deal with these fears, I did ask her why. Why did she want to make this change? What made it worth the dangers and consequences? Would she still want to be (and look like) a man five years from now? Fifteen years from now?

After half a year of thinking about these questions, she said that she felt more comfortable, more at home as a man than as a woman. She felt it was worth the dangers, and that she was convinced that she would continue to want to be a man her entire life. That seemed good. In Eckankar, the religion I practice, I believe in reincarnation. Maybe my daughter had been a man in the most recent past life and hadn't been ready to be reincarnated as a woman in this life. Or maybe there was something he needed to learn by growing up as a female. Looking at it from the perspective of many lives, this was only one life, and he would certainly learn more about love and life from his experiences.

Perhaps illogically, I was a little afraid that more than her body would change after taking testosterone. However, now, after his transition, I realize that he, as a person, has not changed. His personality seems the same, he still hugs me and he hasn't changed his interests.

My son moved to another city and state for his transition. He wanted to have time on his own to adjust and change physically, away from old friends and family. This move was challenging, but seemed to work out for him. Now he has moved back to the San Francisco area. Recently, a friend of mine told me that many young people are accepting of and knowledgeable about transgender people—at least in the area where we live. This made me feel a little better and so far has been largely true, according to my son.

Initially one of my family members was very negative about my son's transition. He looked into studies about people who had transitioned, and he learned that those people felt better and more comfortable about themselves after they transitioned. These studies helped him change his mind. All in all, my friends and family have been supportive of my son. They feel that whatever makes him happy and doesn't hurt others is good.

My son realized he was a man after he had grown up. Coming out as being a man was a big decision for him, but he seems happy with it after several years. I am proud that he did something that he felt so strongly about—even though it was a scary and difficult decision. I had to let him be what he felt he was, and to let go of my own fears around it. Now he looks like the male side of the picture he drew several years ago. To me, his mother, he is still the same soul whom I love.

Rebecca Lewis has a liberal arts degree and lives in the San Francisco Bay Area. She has enjoyed the challenges of learning to fly and to scuba dive. Another great adventure she and her husband did together was having two children, and she took parenting classes to become a better parent. She has studied and practiced Eckankar for forty years. She loves to sing and dance and is a volunteer teacher.

Jim and Kat

Leslie Keeney

My world was drastically changed on a beautiful October Sunday morning. Little did I know that I was about to embark on the most painful, joyous, and educational experience of a lifetime, a journey that not many parents will ever have the privilege of taking.

I'm a mom, a stepmom, a grandma and a great-grandma. I was raised in a fairly strict, white, Catholic home, with members of the clergy and the convent as either relatives or very close family friends. I grew up and came of age in the San Francisco of the sixties, although I was not a flower child. My political views have always leaned towards the conservative, yet I have always appreciated the diverse nature of humanity. I attribute this to growing up in the Bay Area where diversity is a part of life. I never knew how my ability to embrace diversity would one day play such a role in my life, an important role, a vital role.

My father, now deceased, was a retired Naval officer, and, yes, he was a gentleman! My parents divorced when I was young, and my mother raised my two sisters, my brother, and me. And, despite the usual teenage epithets I threw at her, I know she did a good job.

I married at an early age and had two sons who are only thirteen months apart, and was divorced from their police officer father after seven years of marriage. For the first two or three years, it was a fairly amicable divorce; I tried my best to keep it that way for the sake of the boys. After I remarried, things changed, and due to a myriad of circumstances which included a move to southern California, the boys moved in with their father. It was during this time that I became estranged from my children for many years.

The story of our reconciliation begins with a phone call from my oldest son's wife, and ends with a phone call from my youngest son two years later. Reconciling with my children, getting to know their spouses, and being a grandmother brought a sense of completeness and fulfillment that had been missing from my life during the years of our estrangement.

Then came that fateful Sunday morning in a not-too-long-ago October. My husband and I were visiting my youngest son and his family at their home in Texas. We were there for a two-and-a-half week vacation, and the first week had just come to a close. During that week we celebrated my oldest granddaughter's fifth birthday, complete with cupcakes at school and her birthday party on Saturday.

After a water balloon fight with my son, the neighbors, and my granddaughters (who sure know how to throw those balloons with deadly accuracy and explosiveness), we went inside to dry off, change clothes, and rest a bit. My son retreated to the master bedroom to study, as he was finishing his degree, and I settled in front of the computer to drop an email to family and friends to catch them up on our vacation.

As I was doing this, my daughter-in-law came into the study and asked me to come upstairs with her. Thinking that my granddaughters wanted me to join them in playing dolls, I told her that I'd be up in a couple of minutes. She very calmly said, "No, you need to come now." As we headed upstairs my head was reeling, wondering what the problem might be. When we reached the top of the stairs, my daughter-in-law took my arm, stroked it, and said, "You need to be strong."

Immediately, I began imagining the worst. And when I walked into the master bedroom and saw my son sitting on the bed in tears, I was sure he was dying and that I would not be returning home until after I buried my child. As I sat down on the bed, he put my mind to ease by announcing that he was not dying. Those were such beautiful words. But then I was told something that I never thought I would hear in a million years. My son told me that he had struggled with his gender identity for as long as he could remember, and that he was beginning the steps necessary for his transition to being female.

How did I react? I held him, I cried with him, I told him I loved him, I laughed with him, and cried with him some more. Then I started asking questions...questions whose answers helped me to begin to understand the pain that my child had been in for thirty-four years. I learned about the journey that my child was embarking on, and how I could play a valuable role in this journey, even beyond being Mom. That day, my questions and my child's answers started to open my mind and my heart to the issue of being transgender, and also opened to members of the trans community.

I was shocked, as was my husband, as we never had a clue that my son was struggling with his gender identity while growing up. He did all the "boy" things: Scouts, youth football, climbing trees, throwing rocks, building roads in the garden for his model cars and trucks. I realized that he had developed tools at a young age to hide what he was really feeling inside.

From that moment on, I started thinking of my child not as my son, but as my daughter. At her behest, I chose her new, female middle name. I tried to remember *her, she, daughter,* and *Kathryn*—as opposed to *him, he, son,* and *Jim*. I tried to be there for other members of our family—my oldest son, in particular—and to answer questions as honestly and as knowledgeably as I could. Wanting to learn as much as I could, and wanting to get answers to all the questions that were tumbling through my head, I reached out to the Out and Equal group that was one of the many employee interest groups sponsored by my employer. I was put in contact with a delightful young woman who was making her transition. I was able to ask her questions that I did not want to bother my daughter with, and to have the opportunity to talk frankly about some of my fears. (Fears for my daughter's safety were foremost in my mind at the time.) She answered my questions honestly and directly, and she and my daughter have since become fast friends. I consider this very special woman to be a member of my family.

When my child came out as transgender, I had to go

through the same coming out process that all parents of LGBT children go through. I needed to tell family and a few close friends. I thought long and hard about it, and decided that an email to all would be the best way to share our news. Doing that, I knew, would eliminate the phone tree that would start if I called or snail-mailed relatives. And, it would be so much faster, and I could say the same thing to everyone at the same time. I was amazed at how family and friends took the news with the proverbial grain of salt. My mother, who is over eighty years old, simply said, "I've always wanted a granddaughter; now I have one." Our family is easily the most accepting group of people on this earth.

It was fairly easy to come to terms with my daughter's transition. I won't lie and say that I've not cried myself to sleep, thinking of what might have been and how our lives have changed. Nor will I say that I've never encountered prejudice. I've done both. The tears dry; the prejudice…well, I've just distanced myself from those who cannot accept. Those people are the ones who, in the end, may someday regret their preju-dicial viewpoint. Who's to say that they will never have a child come out to them as being a member of the LGBT community?

I worried about my granddaughters. How would they, at ages three and five, handle this change that was about to take place? It is now obvious to me that it is simply not an issue for them. They are happy, well-adjusted little girls who just happen to have two mommies in their house. I also worried about my daughter-in-law. But she is adjusting, and has felt from the beginning that she was put on this earth to help my daughter through her transition. My daughter-in-law truly is a modern-day saint.

The one thing I want more than anything else for my children is happiness. My daughter is truly happy now that she is living the life that she always knew she should be living. The sweetest words I ever heard were from my daughter as she was coming out of anesthesia after her SRS: "Mom, I'm so happy." I will remember those words for the rest of my life.

Finally, I don't look at this as losing a son. Instead, I've gained a daughter, and we have a lot of mother–daughter adventures ahead of us!

Leslie Keeney was born and raised in San Francisco. She is the mother of two, a son and a daughter, as well as step-mom to three. She is a strong ally of the LGBT movement, and is very proud of her daughter for taking the steps to become the person she always knew she should be.

My Son is Ivan Michael

Marie Stouffer

My son is Ivan Michael. He's ten years old. Ivan was born in Siberia. When we adopted Ivan, who is biologically female, her name was Aleksandra.

I'd always anticipated having children, being a mom. I especially hoped for a daughter, envisioning us doing "girl" things: dressing up, playing beauty parlor. Still single at thirty, I started to panic. I became depressed and anxious, fixating on the void in my life. A few years later, I met my now-husband, John. A naval officer, he was stationed in Hawaii and I lived in San Diego. For three years, we maintained a long-distance relationship. Less than a year into our relationship, I was diagnosed with breast cancer. Due to my age, thirty-six, I chose aggressive treatment; the drugs caused early menopause. Because of my history, hormones for fertility treatments were out. I felt more despair and hopelessness than ever before.

John and I married in 2001. We decided to adopt, but were turned down by the first agency. I gave up hope. But John was optimistic, and promised we would make it happen. He said it with such conviction that I believed it. While shopping one day, I saw a little flowered dress. I imagined it on my daughter, and bought it. I hung it on my future daughter's door as a symbol.

In 2003, we were beyond excited to travel to Russia to adopt Aleksandra. Becoming parents had been a rough road; the international adoption process took almost two years of paperwork, red tape, and frustration, and at times we had felt like giving up. When we met our daughter for the first time, our joy was overwhelming. She was undernourished, and small for age two-and-a-half. She had spent her entire life in either the hospital or the orphanage. We were so proud to become her parents.

Early on, we learned that Alex was a tomboy with no interest in playing house or dressing up. She was reckless and preferred wrestling with Dad. So pretty, blue eyed, blonde, and dimpled, we thought she was a cute tomboy.

At about four, she started acting out. She became very defiant. But knowing that behavioral problems are common to post-institutionalized children, we weren't really alarmed. Her behavior became more worrisome, however, when she entered kindergarten. At first we did not link the violence with a gender identity issue, but in retrospect, this should have been a clue. She began to have rages, which she expressed with uncontrollable screaming. Eventually she got violent, destroying property and physically attacking us.

She chose to play mostly with boys; she wanted short hair.

She refused dresses and skirts. Nothing pink nor shiny, not even the tiniest print. She disdained all things "girly-girl." She took drama classes but only wanted the male parts. In pretend play she was the baby boy or the brother. I stopped buying her feminine clothes and trying to fix her hair.

Her behavior problems persisted and escalated through the first and second grades. She was hitting, kicking, even threatening to kill us. She started the couch on fire. I was afraid that she would hurt herself and us. It was a horrible time. Besides worry and fear, I felt self-pity. Not only was I denied my sweet little girl, but our daughter acted like she hated us.

We just wanted to be a family; instead, it was a nightmare. Our marriage suffered and we felt despair. We consulted developmental-behavioral specialists. They acknowledged our gender concerns, but they focused on developmental delays, attachment disorder, and possible fetal alcohol syndrome. We started therapy.

We met with a therapist individually and in various configurations: Alex alone, Alex and I, the three of us together. We worked on strengthening our bond and slowly gaining Alex's trust. We had many emotional talk sessions; the therapist helped us to express our feelings more openly. The therapist combined talk therapy with play therapy; we ended each session with a fun activity: board games, bubble blowing, or pretend play with hand puppets and stuffed animals.

Gradually, over a period of more than a year, Alex became more open with us and started to grasp the idea that we truly loved her and would do anything to help her. Eventually she was able to verbalize her reality. She told us she didn't want to live; she hated the way she looked. She asked Santa for a penis. She longed to pee standing. She said that she felt trapped inside a girl's body. Eventually she stated definitively that she *was* a boy. We came to realize, after researching gender identity disorder, and much soul-searching, that Alex was our son, not our daughter.

That was an extremely painful time, worse than anything I'd dealt with. Although we'd been in denial for some time, John and I were forced to accept that Alex's feelings weren't transitory. Any tiny hope that she would change her mind diminished and died. We were terrified about her future, so we started researching like crazy and made a plan.

On our approaching family vacation, Alex began his transition. The neutral location freed him to dress like a boy and wear short hair. It was a difficult, confusing time for John and me, but the change in our child was profound: the rages subsided, the violence and threats almost completely stopped. Our new reality simultaneously wore me down and built up my hopes for Alex's happiness. I cried every day, but only in private.

Alex's transition continued. He had already chosen a name for himself: Ivan Michael. We felt it was important that we honor his choice, believing that it was central to his identity. We began to use his new name and male pronouns exclusively (although we sometimes slipped and referred to him as *she* or *Alex*). But I was conflicted about this new name. His happiness made me happy, but I had always loved his given name, as well as his middle name, Grace, which we had chosen and was very meaningful to me.

Three years later, I'm thankful for the way things are going with our whole family. Every day we feel lucky to be Ivan's parents. Sometimes I think about how different his life could have been if someone else had adopted him, someone who would not have accepted him for who he is. We believe he knows how much we love him, and that we will do anything for him.

I think I will always feel some small longing for the little girl of my fantasy. But to say I miss my daughter isn't exactly right, because my child was never a girl. When shopping, I avoid the girls' department. Seeing moms with their little girls makes me wistful. But I'm thankful that our family is strong and that we are working through things together.

Last year, Ivan began approaching puberty and received an implant of a hormone-blocking drug called Supprelin. Without estrogen, he will not experience female pubertal development. Puberty can be hellish for a transgender child. Ivan is relieved that for the next few years it won't be looming over his head.

As parents, we're not alone in experiencing dread, sadness, grief, and worry. Nor are we unique in feeling optimism while we watch our child come alive and begin to flourish. It's been amazing to see how much happier, calmer, and more secure he is than he was three years ago.

Recently we had his name legally changed, another milestone and another tug on my heart strings. But I love him even more now, my brave, beautiful son.

Marie Stouffer is married and has one son. In a past life, she worked in music marketing and video game production. Now a homemaker, she and her family live in San Diego, California.

When I Knew

Ann Lynn

Tomboy. That's what we thought she was. Playing with the boys. Always wanting to go without a shirt.

When Tyler was in the fourth grade, we were sitting on her bed, and she handed me a slip of paper with the words "I am gay" written on it. I don't remember feeling surprised. We were a family who discussed a lot of things openly. We were a family in therapy. Her aunt had been gay. We had a lot of gay friends. I told her that it was fine if she was gay, and that I would be supportive of her and of whatever she was or would become.

A week later, as we were again sitting on her bed, she handed me another slip of paper. This one said, "I want to be a boy." Again I told her that I would support whatever was right for her. But this time, I added that maybe there were emotional issues, things that had happened in our family, that might have made her want to be a boy.

I had been struggling for years with Chronic Fatigue Syndrome and depression. Had that made her think being a female was unappealing? When I was sick she'd have "All Sports Days" with her father. Had that made her think being a male looked a whole lot more fun? And the baby that had been born when she was five years old was a boy. Caring for him, of course, took some of my already depleted energy away from her. Did that factor into her feelings?

I didn't share all these thoughts with her then, but reassured her that it would all get worked out, and that she would figure out what was right for her, and that I would support that, whatever it was.

But I worried. Had I made this happen? Had I been a bad parent? Had I not tried hard enough to get over my depression and chronic fatigue? My unconditional support for her being transgender was always shadowed by a worry that I had somehow caused it, and had therefore predestined her for a difficult life.

As the years went by, Tyler continued to dress in boys' clothes, was friends with the girls, but *played* with the guys. To me, she was a miracle, able to relate just as well to males and females, to young and old. She was charismatic, and everyone who knew her, loved her.

One night during the Christmas holidays, when Tyler was in her freshman year of college, our family was going to a play with my mother, who knew nothing of Tyler's gender issue. I suggested that maybe it would make things less complicated if she wore some simple female clothing. It was rare that any of us dressed up. So we dug through our closets and found a dark gray ribbed turtleneck in mine, and a pair of black cotton pants in hers. When she put them on, I thought, "What a beautiful lesbian she would make," and I realize now that I probably wished that that was what she was—a lesbian— thinking it would make her life easier, thinking it would mean I had done nothing wrong.

I guess I thought we could live in that limbo forever. But one summer day after Tyler's junior year of college, as she and I drove home from the swimming pool where she hadn't gone swimming, hadn't even changed out of her shorts and baggy T-shirt, she began to cry and told me that she couldn't appear in a female bathing suit the way she was: almost six foot two, with hairy legs and a masculine bearing.

"People stare at me, Mom," she said. "And they whisper about me." And I finally realized that the magic bubble I thought protected my daughter was fragile and painful in a way I had never understood. With her sense of humor, friendliness, and charm, she had made it look easy.

So a few minutes later, sitting on the sofa, I said to her, "Would you like to start looking into going through the transition?" And it seemed as though a weight was lifted off her shoulders. And, in some ways, it fell onto mine.

I was used to Tyler wanting to be a boy, Tyler dressing like a boy. But Tyler *becoming* a boy: that was different. That really scared me. What if he regretted it? What if something went wrong? What if his personality changed and I began to feel as though I had lost my child forever?

The night before his bilateral mastectomy, as we lay snuggled together on the bed in our hotel room in San Francisco, I asked Tyler what he thought it would be like to go to sleep before the surgery *with* breasts, and then to wake up without them. I expected a long answer that might contain a hint of ambivalence, but instead he said one word, "Awesome."

And that is the spirit with which Tyler woke up and began filming, while still on a morphine drip, a documentary about his transition. Even recovering from surgery, he eagerly wanted to interview me, his haggard mother. I had been filled with so much anxiety about this very moment, so it was a revelation to me to see the joy my child felt over what had just taken place, over what had been removed from his life: two parts of his body that had weighed him down ever since puberty.

A few months later, I got up the courage to tell him how terribly worried I had been that he would regret that moment. He said, in such an offhand way, "Oh, Mom, if I had known you were worried about *that,* I could have told you that would never happen." And that was when I knew, maybe for the first time, that the decision he had made had been, for him, the right one.

Ann Lynn is a poet who lives in Atlanta and teaches writing in schools and in the community. Her poetry chapbook, In the Butterfly House, *was published by Finishing Line Press in 2009. She and her son are writing a memoir about their experiences as a transgender person and the parent of a transgender child.*

What I Didn't Say: Letters From a Mother

Anna Randolph

To the principal of my child's elementary school, gay like me, who said, "It makes me sick to think about what would happen to your child if he came to school in a dress." Though your words stabbed me in the heart, I thank you for your honesty about your inability to protect my child on your playground. I understand that you could not singlehandedly hold up the promise of those welcoming rainbow posters in the front hall and that this was a battle you could not fight. You made me understand that my child would have to wait for a while longer before he could try out his "girl-self" in public.

To the music teacher at the same school, also gay, thank you for casting my child as the Queen of Hearts in the fourth- and fifth-grade production of *Alice in Wonderland*. It was a role he was born for. To be able to be on stage in front of the whole school and community wearing his favorite red gown and black heels, swirling the red cape I knitted with white hearts around the bottom, was such an affirmation of my child who had to leave his "girl-self" literally in the closet every time he walked out the door.

To the pediatrician who thought I was asking for sex reassignment surgery for my ten-year-old: I felt so alone after we met, and wondered, again, if I was crazy. You reminded me, because I always forget, that a boy who wants to dress like a girl is so foreign—and scary—to most people. Though you did not accept *my* expertise about my child, you did call the head of child psychiatry at our local medical school, who, lucky for us, knew something about gender identity in children. He told you that, "this mother is right," and that there may be a need for medical intervention at puberty. Thank you for sending us to him, and for educating yourself. May the next mother who comes to you with her girly boy have an easier time with you.

To my child's other parent: did you know that your boyfriend told our child that he can't "pee like a girl"? You were a lesbian once, and we were partners in life and in bringing this child into the world. We sat in bed with my big belly talking about gender-neutral names for our baby and how we were going to make everything available to him or her and not be limited by gender stereotyping. The day you told me that you would not support our child's love of dresses and all things sparkly was the day our child became a battleground. You took him to Karate class and cut his hair short and talked to your stepdaughter in his presence about how wrong it was that I let him wear dresses. He and I went underground then.

In my house he had dresses and jewelry and could wear what he liked. He had friends who loved him and dressed up with him. I lived in constant fear that you would take him from me. This is what I imagined: on one side of the court, the lesbian single mom who dresses her little boy in girl clothes; on the other, the heterosexual couple who know what "normal" is. "Yes, your honor, my child loves to wear dresses and I believe in and support his right to express himself as he likes. No, he is not too young to know what feels right for him."

To the sixth-grade teacher I met with before my child entered your school: you are so far the only one who has made me cry, in one of my attempts at educating the people who will be involved with my child. Thank you for your bluntness and not holding back your opinion that there is no way a child this young can know what he wants to wear. I learned from you that even this new liberal school was no safer than anywhere else. It was clear my child should not be in your classroom.

This was a blessing, because he went to the other teacher instead, a wonderful man who, on the last day of sixth grade, wore his Utilikilt to school. I am glad you retired last year because I can't see how one with so little respect for a parent can work with their children. To your attacks that implied I was a monster for talking about letting my child wear a dress to school, I replied through my angry and unwanted tears that I have a Master's Degree, I am not stupid, I have been parenting this child ever since he was born and know that she is happiest when allowed to be fully herself.

Did you think this was some weird whim I pulled out of my hat? Did you think I was a sick person who wanted my son to be a girl? Did you think I did not love my child and want what's best for him? That I haven't thought about the issues you raised already a hundred times, or done my research? Couldn't you see that I was asking for your help in being on the side of a child who needed your compassion and understanding?

To transgender adults that have grown up in times before now: thank you for your courage in standing up for yourselves. Your stories of oppression and of violence against you, of alienation by others and of the feelings of alienation within your own bodies have made me passionate about educating myself and others about what my child needs to grow up healthy and safe. They inspire me to change the little piece of the world that I can, so that my child can thrive. Thank you for sharing your stories so I could better understand my child.

One of the most significant validations I received for my advocacy of my child's freedom to express his gender identity was when I read transwoman Jennifer Finney Boylan's memoir. She told a story of being three years old watching her mom iron her dad's shirts. Her mom said to her little boy, "Someday you will wear shirts like these," to which Jenny internally replied, "No, I won't." She saw herself wearing women's clothes and growing up to be a woman, not a man. At age three, my little boy said to me that he was not going to grow up to be a man; she was going to grow up to be "a mommy." At the time, I was not sure whether this was just an identification with mommy that many kids have at that age. I now know that she was speaking her truth.

To transgender adults who have communicated to me that since I had not let her transition earlier I was not being accepting of my child: I want to tell you that my child is not growing up in the same world you did. I want you to know that I am committed to helping her live freely in her affirmed gender, whatever it may be. I am also passionately opposed to forcing my child into a decision that neither of us are ready for and that could have a potentially negative impact on her life. Even if it is true, it is not helpful to me when you say to me "your child is transgender" without knowing anything about us. It has been implied that I am harming, even abusing, my child by not letting her transition at age nine or ten. You do not know or bother to ask about our circumstances, or attempt to understand why I make the choices I do. You do not see the many ways I convey my love and acceptance to my child while keeping her safe. You are not responsible for every aspect of this child's well being, as I am.

To other parents of kids like mine: thank you for sharing your thoughts and struggles and triumphs. I respect the different ways we have chosen to respond to our children. There is no easy answer or "right" way to do this job of parenting. I spend many hours reading, listening to other parents, and consulting with professionals as I make decisions on this journey, but ultimately this is between my child and me.

Before I could let my child transition, I needed to know she was in a relatively safe school and neighborhood. I had to assemble a strong team of providers, including a supportive pediatrician, psychiatrist, therapist, and endocrinologist. It was essential that we had a supportive community around us, including a welcoming church, family, and friends. More than anything, I needed my child to be sure she was ready. I believe she has always felt this way, but was unable to claim her identity until she felt support from her other parent, and felt safe enough and strong enough to handle the hard stuff.

To my mother, who told me when I was twenty-one how hard it is to be a lesbian, and that no one would want me around their kids, and that I should keep it quiet at my job at a summer camp, and that lesbians have unstable relationships and unhappy lives: I understand the heart-stopping terror of seeing your child on a path fraught with more than the usual amount of struggle and danger. I know what it is like to hear stories of shootings in classrooms, and crucifixions on rural fences, and suicides of bullied gay and trans youth, and know that that child could be my child. I understand that you were scared for your young lesbian daughter setting off into the world. But what you did not understand was that it was not my choice. Trust me, I would not have chosen to be a second-class citizen, prohibited from marrying the one I love or receiving her Social Security benefits if she dies before me.

I know my child has not chosen this path; it simply is her path. This child let me know who she was the minute she could make her fashion preferences known. I know you loved me, Mom, and wanted me to be okay, but you saw conforming as the way to acceptance. I'm not sure you ever understood that the challenge I felt was not so much due to the fact that I was a lesbian, but that I did not have your support and understanding. May my child always know that I love him just as she is, and that I will always do my best to provide her a safe place to be herself, while I work to change the world. The twenty-one-year-old me would never have imagined that my mother could now call my son by his girl name, and has invited her to come dressed as she likes to parties amongst all her friends. Things change, and I am grateful.

To my partner: thank you for your unwavering support

for us both. Neither of us ever doubt your fierce commitment to us, and we know that we can always count on you as our ally and advocate. Thank you for having a real relationship with this child who did not spend the first ten years of her life with you. I know this is never easy or simple—my child is chaos incarnate with her anxiety and ADHD, her flamboyance, drama, and irritability. You hang in there through all of this, and are still open to the sweet stuff—the homemade earrings labored over for your birthday, the sharing of clothes, her declarations of love and exuberant hugs, and her heart-to-heart talks about things she can't discuss with me. You have courageously joined forces with me in the daunting task of rearing my child and yours together. Thank you for this chance to be a new kind of family.

To my child: walking into the building with you that day of sixth grade when you wore your little white sweater dress to school for the first time was one of the most terrifying moments of my life. You faltered at the door, and I took your hand firmly and walked with you to your classroom. May you always know I have that strength for you when you need it. I am proud to be your mother, and I love the person you are becoming—a brave and tenderhearted beautiful human being.

Anna Randolph is a licensed counselor by profession and lives with her partner and two kids on the edge of adolescence in Portland, Oregon.

Glossary

Bilateral Mastectomy: Surgery to remove both breasts, as in the transition of a female person to male.

Biological sex: Biological sex refers to the sex assigned to a person at birth based on their anatomical presentation.

Gender Identity Disorder: A term used by mental health and medical clinicians, gender identity disorder is still defined as a pathology in many professional reference books, including the influential Diagnostic and Statistical Manual of Mental Disorders (DSM). There is currently a concerted effort underway among gender specialists to have this term removed and/or changed.

Gender variant/gender nonconforming/gender creative:
These often interchangeable terms are used primarily for children and youth who do not follow the expected gender roles or styles of dress expected of their assigned birth sex. For example, a boy who wishes to wear a dress to school may be gender creative, or a girl who insists on only wearing boys swim trunks to the pool may be considered gender nonconforming. Being gender variant, gender non-conforming or gender creative is not necessarily an indication that a child will grow up to be gay or transgender, although this is very often the case. These categories can also be applied to adults who buck traditional gender roles, hair styles, styles of dress, and any other traditional marker of gender.

Hormone blockers: Hormone blockers have become an increasingly common medical protocol for transgender-identified youth. The ones most widely cited, including in this book, are: SUPPRELIN LA, a tube-like implant placed just under the skin on the upper arm, which lasts for about 12 months, or Lupron DEPOT, which is delivered by injection, usually every month or every three months. Originally these drugs were prescribed for children who had very early, pre-pubertal development of secondary sex characteristics. These drugs are now becoming widely known as hormone blockers for transgender children, given between the ages of 11-16, as a way to buy time and delay the puberty of their birth sex until further decisions can be made about transition. Research is limited, but most current anecdotal accounts suggest that youth who begin hormone blockers do usually go on to more fully transition.

SRS, or Sex Reassignment Surgery: SRS is a term for the surgical procedures that transgender people have to realign their bodies with their gender identity. Despite what is generally thought, not all transpeople have SRS.

Tanner Stage 2: There are five developmental stages in this widely known medical model of pubertal changes. Tanner Stage 2 is the stage where youth typically begin to receive drugs called hormone blockers that disallow the pubertal development of their birth sex.

Transgender: An individual whose gender identity does not match their assigned birth sex. Having a transgender identity does not depend on whether a person takes hormones or physically alters their body, although many transgender identified people do. Transgender people can be children, teenagers, and adults of any age.

Transition: To live as the opposite gender of the one you were born as, whether or not you physically alter your body with surgery or take cross hormones. In young children who have not reached puberty, often this is called "social transition."

Resource Guide

Advocacy:

Family Acceptance Project
familyproject.sfsu.edu

Gender Spectrum Education and Training
genderspectrum.org

Laura's Playground
lauras-playground.com

Mermaids
mermaidsuk.org.uk

My Princess Boy website
myprincessboy.com

PFLAG
pflag.org

TransFamily of Cleveland
transfamily.org

Transforming Family
transformingfamily.org/about-us

Transgender Law and Policy Institute
transgenderlaw.org

Transgender Law Center
transgenderlawcenter.org/cms

Transgender Psychology Alliance
transgenderpsychologyalliance.org

Trans Kids Purple Rainbow
transkidspurplerainbow.org

TransYouth Family Allies
imatyfa.org

Medical:

Children's Hospital Los Angeles
childrenshospitalla.org
Transgender Services 323-361-2390

Children's National Medical Center, DC
Gender and Sexuality Psychosocial Programs
childrensnational.org

Dimensions Clinic San Francisco
dimensionsclinic.org

GeMS Clinic Children's Hospital Boston
childrenshospital.org

Jim Collins Foundation
jimcollinsfoundation.org

Books:

Becoming a Visible Man by Jamison Green

Gender Outlaws: The Next Generation edited by Kate Bornstein
and S. Bear Bergman

Helping Your Transgender Teen: A Guide for Parents by Irwin
Krieger

My Name is J by Cris Beam

She's Not There: A Life in Two Genders by Jennifer Finney
Boylan

Testosterone Files by Max Wolf Valerio

*Trans Forming Families: Real Stories About Transgendered Loved
Ones, 2nd Edition* edited by Mary Boenk

The Transgender Child: A Handbook for Parents and Professionals
by Stephanie Brill and Rachel Pepper

Resource Guide

Transgender Emergence: Therapeutic Guidelines for Working With Gender-Variant People and Their Families by Arlene Istar Lev

Transgender Explained For Those Who Are Not by Joanne Herman

Transgender History by Susan Stryker

About the Editor

RACHEL PEPPER is a therapist who specializes in working with the transgender community and with the families of transgender and gender nonconforming children and youth. She is also a highly trained practitioner in the field of eating disorders. Rachel holds a Masters in Counseling and also a Masters in Journalism. She is an award-winning, widely published journalist, and a frequent contributor to both fiction and non-fiction anthologies. She is the author or co-author of three previous books, including *The Ultimate Guide to Pregnancy for Lesbians*, *The Gay and Lesbian Guide to College Life*, and *The Transgender Child: A Handbook for Families and Professionals*. Rachel lives with her family in the San Francisco Bay Area. She can be reached directly at RLPepper@hotmail.com.